# *Arm Around Shoulder/ Hand Over Mouth*

## *10 Loving Lessons for Mothers & Daughters-in-law*

# By Mimi Moseley

*Arm Around Shoulder/ Hand Over Mouth*
*10 Loving Lessons for Mothers & Daughters-in-law*
by Mimi Moseley

Printed in the United States of America

ISBN 978-1-60791-211-8

Unless otherwise indicated, Bible quotations are taken from The Ryrie Study Bible, New American Standard Translation® (NASB), Copyright © 1976, 1978 by The Moody Bible Institute of Chicago, and *The Message,* Copyright © 1993, 1994, 1995, 1996, 2000, 2001, 2002, Used by permission of NavPress Publishing Group, and *The Holy Bible, New International Version*, Copyright © 1973, 1978, 1984 by International Bible Society, Used by permission Zondervan.

www.xulonpress.com

*T*his book is dedicated to the precious memory of my mother-in-law, Jean Moseley. And to my two amazing daughters-in-law, Anna and Rebecca. I am book-ended between these and most blessed.

# ACKNOWLEDGEMENTS

My darling husband, Marty, I thank you for all your patience, love and support as I grunted through this process. Here's to where we were yesterday, where we are today and where we will be tomorrow. Please God.

Rebecca and Anna Moseley, you two are the most amazing daughters-in-law I could have ever hoped for. Thank you for helping round out the work Jean began on her end by loving me through the ropes as a new mother-in-law. I love you both so much and I pray I will "walk the talk" of this book in your lives.

Carleen Carver, my dear friend. Thank you for listening to the Holy Spirit and encouraging me to see this through to completion. All the emails when I was at my lowest kept me moving forward.

The POS writers' group: Wanda Puder, Sherry Cox, Ellen Cohen, Jane Baker and Laurie Nemec. I appreciate your welcoming me into the "writers' world" and confirming my calling to write through your words and great editing. To Lisa Bogart who tirelessly encouraged, edited and just plain made me smile behind the scenes. You are a peach! And to Ethel Herr: my deepest appreciation for your confidence in me when I had none. I never thought I would be able to see this through after Jean died, but you spoke truth into my life and spurred me on. I am amazed how the Lord has used you to form me into a writer through your mentoring. When I think of a Titus two woman, I see you. Thank you for your sensitivity and love to me all these years.

To Stefan Wiechers who willing stepped forward to take just the right photo for the back cover when all others had tried and given up.

Finally, I thank the Lord who ultimately wrote this book. You lovingly reached through my broken-heart after Jean's death and sweetly revealed to me the agreement with you to write this book is what a "calling" looks like. You showed me greater dimensions of knowing you as the Author and Finisher as I surrendered this effort to you. Take it, Lord. Use it to your glory. May women praise you for any benefits this book brings.

# TABLE OF CONTENTS

# FOREWORD
## By Ethel Herr – Christian Writer & Speaker

Some of the most treacherous of our relationship journeys we travel in this life are those we share with in-laws. Marriage can be tough—maybe tougher—because it is intimate and so always-present, inescapable. And parenting!! Well, yes those both top the list of toughies.

But in-lawing comes right alongside, and happens in conjunction with both marriage and parenting. It has its own set of difficulties and complexities, enough to drive one to do foolish, regrettable, and sometimes desperate things.

I had a good mother-in-law, my mother was a good mother-in-law. So we all got off to a good start in this household. Basically my children chose mates I can usually get along with. But we have had stumbling stones along the way. I entered marriage convinced that I had the most nearly ideal situation on earth. After all, we all loved Jesus, so what could go wrong? Oh my, it didn't take long for me to discover that no journey is perfect.

When Mimi married Marty Moseley, she knew all the bad press about in-laws. However, God had a most remarkable and pleasant surprise in store for her. For every reason she could think of, her mother-in-law should not like her or accept her, certainly not love her. But then, Jean Moseley, was not your ordinary mother-in-law.

Mimi and I have gotten acquainted over the writing of this book. I have learned all about Mimi's lack of preparation for life and marriage. With awe, I watched the story unfold. Jean opened her heart to the little waif her son brought to her to love, and made loving just the starting point.

Often as we've worked our way through this book I've realized that every young bride has so much more to learn than she has any idea. So does every new mother-in-law. I've felt the inadequacy from both sides, and had to draw on all the resources of heaven to bring me up to speed. I can honestly say God has been consistently faithful to teach me — often through my mother-in-law or a daughter-in-law, even a son-in-law. Come to think of it, I believe I learned a few things from my father-in-law as well.

During the truly hard years in our home, when we took my mother-in-law in as a member of the family, all our goodwill toward one another was tested to the ultimate point. How often I would have given anything in the world to have had Mimi's book in hand. So much she says here was exactly what I craved to hear.

"Admittedly," says Mimi in her introduction, "this topic of in-law relationships will spark pain in many. It may even bring afresh a hidden sense of rejection or absence of love." But that's not where it stops. This book can also take even the most pained of us and give us new hope for the steps that lie ahead. Mimi and Jean teamed up in learning to live and love and now in helping the rest of us to understand some highly practical ways to handle our personal struggles to do the same. Mimi hides nothing in giving us examples so convincing that we believe that the motto Jean taught her can really, truly work! "Arm around shoulder... hand over mouth."

You, the reader of this book, are about to be blessed big time. And I know long before you come to the end, you will join me in saying to the wonderful women who created it, "Thank you Mimi and Jean! And thank You God!"

# INTRODUCTION

"*I hate my mother-in-law!*" I've heard this painful comment too many times from the mouths of young women. There are jokes about mothers-in-law and recently there was a movie in the theaters on the ever increasing contention between mothers and their children's spouses. It is the discord which fuels many an afternoon television talk show.

I am often asked, "Do I just accept this relationship is strained or can I do something?" I dialogued this very mystery years ago with my mother-in-law, Jean Moseley, leading to our decision to write this book on loving in-laws. Was there enough encouraging wisdom in our shared experiences to help break this cycle of self-fulfilling misery? Looking back on our almost thirty years as daughter and mother-in-law, we decided yes, indeed there was.

Jean and I are card-carrying Pollyannas. *Pollyanna,* for those unfamiliar, was a Disney movie of the 60's: The old story of an orphaned young girl that comes to live with her stoic grandmother offering propriety over love following the untimely death of her parents. Even in her sorrow, Pollyanna made choices to find something to be thankful for everyday. This ray of sunshine in a gray world of ambivalence grated on the nerves of everyone around her, but her perseverance paid off. In the end, her sweet spirit became contagious to all and produced an epidemic of thankful hearts.

Jean adopted a "Pollyanna" attitude early in life which I have come to claim as well. Her decision to search for the good around her and to be thankful everyday resulted in a woman of kindness and wisdom. Over time, her example of thankfulness eventually rubbed off on me. Even though, the many opportunities for a grateful heart I foolishly missed, my mother-in-law's determination modeled a spirit of God's grace resulting in loving lessons on how to love an in-law.

We acknowledge that all issues cannot be resolved with a sweet smile and positive thinking. Admittedly, even discussing the topic of in-law relationships could spark pain in many and may even bring afresh a hidden sense of rejection or absence of a love desired.

A first hand viewing of the desperation and hopelessness in women drove Jean and me to prayer. What was missing in the lives of these women? Was it simply a "thankful heart"? Of course not! Love was missing. There are over fifteen "one anothers" in the New Testament that encourage love and acceptance in all relationships, plus many more passages concerning what to do when conflicts arise. God did not place us in this world to go it alone and He is not unaware of the in-laws in our lives.

*"And now I ask you, lady, not as though I were writing to you a new commandment, but the one which we have had from the beginning, that we love one another."* 2 John 1:5

The Apostle John's message contained no new revelation. It was a reminder of Jesus' words to *continue* loving one another. Love is clear when shown and obvious when counterfeited.

Another of Jesus' apostles, Paul, gave a mandate from God in Titus 2:3-5. Written to all women it states that the older woman is to encourage the younger to love their husbands and children, be kind and sensible so that the word of God may not be dishonored. From God's Word we learn His instructions are to reach out to the younger women and help them down the road the older ones have already traveled.

Jean and I did not and do not pretend to have any training other than what we had learned through Scripture and the life lessons the Lord has taught us in loving. Nor do we profess to make light of seriously damaged relationships. We are just two Southern gals convinced a heart searching for God's direction through His inspired Word and by using some tried and true tools, has nothing to lose.

We also wrote this book to offer some pro-active steps to begin and nurture loving relationships not only between mothers and daughters-in-law, but also in every aspect of interaction among women. This is *not* a "how to" book, but a "you have a choice" book. Maybe, a Pollyanna attitude might help you begin your effort to merely survive with that in-law, but we pray you will gain the courage to cultivate the fallow (unfruitful) ground into productive soil for God's garden.

October 11, 2005 Jean stepped away from this book project and into Glory. I did not believe I could continue this effort without her. Just as these pages will point you to Jesus, her memory pointed me to Him for confirmation to continue. Short of a Gideon experience with fleeces, I saw His hand moving and His direction to carry on. Jean left a mark on my life as you will see woven throughout these pages. She bestowed a legacy, if you will, to me and eventually to my two daughters-in-law through the loving lessons of *Arm Around Shoulder/Hand Over Mouth*. I pray you know the love and acceptance we have found in Jesus is available to you and in turn see how you can show it to others. It is in Christ alone we put our trust and in Christ alone we pray you seek to be encouraged in your in-law relationships. What have you got to lose?

# Lesson 1

# *Little Things Matter*

Most conflicts start over little things that could have easily been fixed had someone made the effort. Herb Kelleher, co-founder and CEO of Southwest Airlines intentionally asked employees what could make their work more comfortable. It came down to the simple request: The ticket agents were not concerned with more high tech equipment, their feet hurt. Hearing the problem alone was not solving it. Tired feet may not seem like a big deal, but Kelleher believed if he could head off the little issues they might not grow into major ones. His solution was to put a pad under the agents' feet. It took determination but asking the agents' feedback allowed him to head off problems which honored him as a boss who cares.

We've all heard sayings like, "dealing with the little stuff as it arises is most beneficial", while others say "Don't sweat the small stuff." Jean believed as

Kelleher *little things matter* and practiced this lesson often with me. She told me Jesus was concerned with the little things, too. Not just the affairs of the world, but with my every thought. Did that mean parking places, finding lost car keys as well as peace in time of crisis? Jean believed so and now, so do I. Christ is very interested in what interests me and wants to coach me through His Holy Spirit to make my requests known to Him in prayer. The sovereign God does not *need* me to tell Him my problems. I *need* to bring them to Him as an agreement I'm not the Answerer.

Here's an example: I have a pair of jeans I loved. I just couldn't get into them. Those jeans were not expensive or terribly fashionable, but I loved them nonetheless because they fit. When my size graduated to the height of my weight gain, I refused to let a few extra pounds force me into the next size which came with an elastic waist. I went to work exercising, made some progress then celebrated my lost half pound with spinach dip. You can see where this is going.

Again and again I fought, won and celebrated, only to be rewarded with the merry-go-round emotions of defeat and discouragement. Jean suggested I ask the Lord for help. This seemed foolish since I munched my way out of those jeans, why would Jesus be interested in my self-centered request to lose weight when marriages were failing and cancer was at an all time high? No, what I needed was a personal trainer!

I happened to be reading in Philippians at the time and surprisingly ran across just such a Trainer. I discovered His "*let's get started*" message to me.

"*Let your gentleness be known to all. The Lord is near. Do not be anxious about anything, but in everything, by prayer and petition, with thanksgiving present your requests to God.*" Philippians 4:5-6 (New International Version)

Did He say *everything?* I can even take something little like dieting to Him? Absolutely! My self-reliance overshadowed the truth of God's willingness. This lack of readiness was not only reflected in my weight gain, but also in my spiritual attitude. God's Word had confronted me on an issue I did not think He would care about. I needed to invite Him into my diet struggle the same as any other struggle in my life. He is indeed interested. My presumption this was something I needed to handle without God, declared I knew better than He. I had settled on a line that distinguished what was mine to accomplish and what was God's. He wanted that line removed. I took a deep breath and chose to surrender. My new prayer became, "*Lord, train my heart to seek you in all things, even weight loss.*" Jesus is the qualified Personal Trainer. He is concerned when I am out of sorts and wants me to take my burdens to Him with thanksgiving for my membership in His gym.

We all have those "lines in the sand", or little things we may not feel worthy of giving to God.

Where are your lines? What little things do you keep your ruling hand on? Oh, we desperately cling to God when we learn of an undiagnosed illness in a child. Or what about the look on the doctor's face when the test results come back? We are quick to fall at the feet of Jesus for these mysteries which can only be changed by the movement of God's hand. Strangely, we may confuse the level of His love and desire to meet us when the struggle is something smaller. The old adage, "Pick yourself up by your bootstraps" creeps in and we mistakenly move ourselves to the position of sovereign.

How about the "little things" with your in-law? This is not a life and death issue, but it causes your heart to ache and your emotions to rule, doesn't it? Have you tried and failed so often in your own power, you just accept the next size elastic pants? It will never improve, why try? How about judging small things as not worthy of your concern with comments like *"Oh, I don't know why that is such a big deal to my in-law. It's such a little thing. She should get over it!"* Jesus says to seek Him in *all* things and Paul reminds us to buffet our bodies and minds in submission to Christ. It's gonna take effort.

Some of us have ignored little issues with in-laws so long a weight gain of disconnect has resulted and we give up ever achieving a "fit". We are aware the relationship is not healthy, exercise is needed!

Have I got the Trainer for you! He'll meet you at this admission you need training. He won't rush you, but will begin your routine with a warm up then moving you to renewed strength to work the cardio-an improvement of the heart; to the perfect finish; a body of spiritual health. He is the Author and Finisher of our faith as well as our soul's body builder. Always near, He knows exactly how far He can stretch us in this exercise program.

Jean, not the pants but the mother-in-law, was great in dealing with little issues from the time I met her. As sweet and gentle as she was, she had a healthy sense of right and wrong which she was not afraid to share with the graciousness of her Southern charm. Because she had made the life exercise choice to embrace and watch out for the little things God had for her in His training program, He brought opportunities for daily stretching. I was one of those stretching opportunities. Here's my story:

I had been dating Marty over a year when I moved to Tennessee to be closer to him, leaving my home and secret past in Atlanta. Had I been required to produce a quality resume for future daughters-in-law, mine would never be chosen. I grew up the youngest child of alcoholic parents. At the tender age of 17, my parents divorced. I could not imagine how my short life could be worse, but less than two years later my world stopped with a phone call. My father had died of cirrhosis of the liver in a hotel room on a business trip. Devastated, confused and alone, suicidal thoughts became my constant companion. *This life stinks! I want out!* My sense of security and lack of control spiraled down into a pit of shame and loneliness. My daddy was supposed to provide for, love and protect me. Now what? Who could I rely on? I felt trapped in a world I could not control and desperate for help. Though a voice whispered in my ear to end it all, my cowardice won out. Despondent, yet determined, I put on a happy face and hid pain.

Like many adult children of alcoholics, I shared a flawed characteristic in my quest for survival-*don't let anyone see you sweat the small stuff.* If only I can look good to the world with a "mind over matter" attitude, I will survive. I hid my painful past behind a beautiful, well painted mask and walked into Jean's world.

Unsuspectingly, Jean received and thought of me as a sweet girl from Atlanta. My camouflage held well until I received news from home a few months later my mother had shot and killed herself. Mom seemed to have no cowardice toward suicide and ended her life with gruesome finality. I was left at 21, crushed to the core. My disguise shattered like a two-way mirror suddenly allowing my ugly truth to be seen. Exposed! No longer could I hide my secret family life. I became frantic envisioning this new opportunity for life in Tennessee slipping through my fingers. How could Marty's family accept someone like me now? I would lose for sure. I stood uncovered and fearful. Was failure my lot? Would they abandon me, too? Marty and I had talked of marriage but I wondered would he still want someone so damaged? Amazingly, he did still want me, and a few months later we shared our marriage plans with his parents. Let me pause to tell you I prayed over two decades for the women who would become my sons' wives. I wanted nothing but the best for them. Had a "Mimi" come along, I would have told them to run fast and far away from that girl. As a matter of fact, there were one or two I did caution them about, but I had been much worse than any girl my boys ever brought home. As I think back, had I walked in Jean's shoes, I would have stopped Marty cold with the old cliché, "Sweetie, the fruit don't fall far from the tree". An obvious concern would be: she could become an alcoholic. "Gee, son, she could even be suicidal! We don't really know her. How about a nice girl from Tennessee?"

Who would have blamed Jean if she had those same fears and warned Marty to flee? This was not a little thing and I was certainly not what Jean had pictured when imagining her precious baby boy's future. She had done nothing to earn this new weight yet my presence packed invisible pounds on her.

Surprisingly, she did not warn Marty. Instead, she humbly sought the Lord who had just dumped a lifelong calling on her and asked, "What are you going to do, Jean?" She gave up voting rights and chose Christ to train her heart, mind and body to His good purpose.

As a "card carrying" Pollyanna, Jean looked for some way she could practice thankfulness as she sought God through this calling. Perhaps she *might* have said, "Well, I can be thankful Mimi has not been in jail, killed anyone or carries a weapon. She doesn't seem to have any tattoos and I think her hair color is naturally blonde." Hmmm, with that let's move on with the story...

Like me, Jean had also prayed for her sons. I recall her saying all she asked the Lord for were wives who loved her sons deeply and faithfully. This was one simple little thing that mattered a lot to her. She never dreamed she may have needed to be more specific in her wish list for the dream daughter-in-law. Her dream soon turned into a nightmare. God's "calling" on Jean was not to be a missionary or a Sunday school teacher, but to lay down her will to Jesus, take up her cross and follow Him with this new charge.

Jean began a mission to pray for me, another seemingly little thing, and asked God to grant her the ability to model a godly life and then the wisdom to live out "arm around shoulder, hand over mouth". Little did she know what a handful I would be?

At the time, Jean had been reading the first chapter of the book of James. It begins with the admonition to:

> "*Consider it all joy, my brethren, when you encounter various trials.*" James 1:2

I don't think Jean was feeling very joyful in this calling. I was headstrong and not easy to love. Thankfully, she did not stop at verse two but read on,

> "*knowing that the testing of your faith produces endurance. And let endurance have its perfect result, that you may be perfect and complete, lacking in nothing.*" James 1:3-4

Some Bible translations use the word "patience", but I like the New American Standard Bible's use of "endurance" which was much more applicable. Unsuspectingly, Jean had 28 years of endurance ahead of her for this choice to let the Lord train her in His gym. He had begun the training with important little things that tested and strengthened her to follow in the path the Lord had set and obediently prayed.

Obedience is all well and good, but exactly what was she supposed to do besides pray? She had no experience counseling an adult orphan. Thankfully, Jean was still in the book of James as the Lord built on His own words to direct her steps. I can almost hear Him saying, "Step One: KEEP READING!"

*"But if any of you lacks wisdom, let him ask of God, who gives to all men generously and without reproach, and it will be given to him. But let him ask in faith without any doubting."*
James 1:5 – 6a

The Lord would not ridicule Jean for not knowing what to do but would welcome her request for His wisdom. The sovereign God had brought me to her and now called her to seek Him in praying for this wildcat. She had been faithful in the small things of her life and now was granted a big one.

*"Whoever can be trusted with very little can also be trusted with much."* Luke 16:10a (NIV)

27

Jean did not deserve the care set before her. She stood on the edge of an unsure future and committed to the Lord to faithfully pray. She made a choice to heal from her own disappointments and then made the choice to see His purpose through her "trial", me. Jean practiced with her arm around my shoulder and her hand over her mouth. It took years, and neither of us is exactly sure when it happened, but one day she became my best friend and mother and I became her daughter.

Jean had taken a glimpse of my troubled young life and found a little thing to motivate her. I was a girl all alone and needed her. I believe this contributed to her compassion toward me, allowing her to offer grace for all the times I struggled. I had some successes which kept her going, but often failed at some of the same lessons she hoped I had learned.

Most of us don't know what has gone on in the family lives of others. Yet as in-laws we mistakenly assume we will all live happily ever after and others will adjust as they buy into the family. We see surface reactions and may respond emotionally rather than making the choice to consider what might be the root of our in-law's actions. Could a daughter-in-law be jealous her own family is not like the husband's family? Maybe there was a divorce or abuse or some other history of dysfunction. Or maybe a mother-in-law sees the young bride as more materialistic than she? What may be commonplace to one generation might look like irresponsibility to another. Take a moment to find a little thing to help understand why your in-law is the way she is, or one thing that is important to her to focus on so she knows her feelings matter.

Like Jean, God may be placing a "Mimi" in your life in the form of an in-law. He is not calling you to "fix" that person but to seek Him. Go on, call to Him. He is near.

*"For the eyes of the Lord move to and fro throughout the earth that He may strongly support those whose hearts are truly His."* II Chronicles 16:9

Throughout history, it has been His desire to seek His people, draw them near and listen for their voices. He's ready to step in, ready to support, and He invites us to call with promises like:

*"Call to Me, and I will answer you and I will tell you great and mighty things, which you do not know."* Jeremiah 33:3

*"Answer me when I call, O God of my righteousness! Thou hast relieved me in my distress; be gracious to me and hear my prayer."* Psalm 4:1

I ask, "Does the little stuff matter?" Maybe like me, a private session with the Personal Trainer Jesus, is in order? Of course getting use to being concerned with the little things will take work. A new exercise regimen requires the preparation of a new attitude, the determination to practice and the resolve to endure.

Keep your focus and remember not only do you have the Owner of the gym, the Trainer and Fitness Coordinator in the form of the Trinity cheering you on, but a great cloud of witnesses as well who know little things do indeed matter. (Hebrews 12:1)

## Lesson 2

# *Everybody Can Be a "So-'n-So", So Watch Yourself!*

The old cliché "so-'n-so" usually refers to a self-serving person who is bossy or in my words just acts like a jerk. If asked, many of us could readily pull up a list of people who, through their actions, qualifies them for such a title. Rarely, do we concede any shortcomings of our own to be on anyone's list. Yet, there we are.

I wasn't the first "so-'n-so" in Jean's life. Early in Jean's marriage she visited her friend Annelle Miller's home. Annelle, always the charming Southern belle, listened patiently to Jean rant about her new husband's ways, then gently touched Jean's hand and said, "Dahlin', everybody can be a "so-'n-so." Wow, what a mountain of wisdom her little phrase embodied. Annelle's comment offered understanding, compassion and perseverance with words as gentle as her touch. Jean's husband, Martin, was no different than other husbands or any different than any of us. We are all capable of trying the patience of another.

Jean told me the truth of those profound words began her resolve of "arm around shoulder, hand over mouth" which guarded her from expressing negative attitudes by remaining silent long enough to show love first. A silence which enabled her to hear the true needs of another.

This spilled out not only to her husband but to friends, students and strangers. Jean's "love first" decision allowed plenty of opportunities for clemency to friends and family members who seemed to take turns claiming the "so-'n-so" title. Once, Jean's father had been in a foul mood all day and went to bed grumpy. The following morning, in an effort to start the day better, her mother greeted him with a bright smile and a hearty breakfast. She was rewarded with the same grump she saw the day before. Indignant, Jean's mother said, "Oh, no you don't! You got to be ornery yesterday. Today is my turn!" A funny story, but one that speaks the truth of our nature...*it's all about us.*

I encountered my first memorable "so-'n-so" at a week-long summer cheer-leading camp in high school. I'm sure the name I gave her back then was stronger than "so-'n-so". With only a few ill-chosen words, this fellow team member painfully dissolved the atmosphere of unity the camp experience was meant to promote spinning me out of orbit with feelings of isolation and shunning. Her careless, yet typical, teenage remarks struck deeper than she could have ever known. Granted, she was tacky in her manner and may have spoken intentionally, but that's just the way some people are. If you attended high school in America, you probably found yourself on the receiving end of insensitive comments, too.

Before we judge her too quickly, let's look a little closer at the situation. She came from a good home with a healthy family environment. She had no idea what went on in my home since I never let anyone get close enough to know my pain. She may even have perceived my evasive behavior regarding my family, and the fact no one was ever invited to my house, as superiority on my part. This young gal did not know the fear I carried about my true home life being discovered. Cheer-leading was my escape. For a few sweet hours each week, and for a precious five days in the summer, I could appear normal just like everyone else. This girl did not know what she did not know and could not comprehend how her words reinforced my feelings of unworthiness or ever being normal.

In a continuing effort to survive, *my* response was a choice to become tacky myself. "Hurt others before they hurt you" seemed my fitting mantra. For a while, I judged and criticized with the worst of them, and hated myself more and more for the ugly person I was becoming. I thought if I made others look small I might look better. As a new Christian, I knew the Lord was not pleased but I excused my actions and claimed I had just cause due to my lot in life. I had a right to be a "so-'n-so".

It was an unfair world I lived in at this early age and I resented the wake of pain and shame I experienced due to my parents' choices. I was an angry victim claiming, *"I didn't bring this on! If other's had gone through what I did, they would be even worse!"* But try as I might, I could not justify my new attitude. I was miserable and quickly shed the cloak of pain inflictor. I pledged not to be the initiator of misery to anyone else regardless of my hurt. Oh, but once the "so-'n-so" demon gets a hook in you, it is hard to tame and can easily slip out again.

A "so-n-so" slipped out early in my marriage. Marty and I headed to Tennessee for vacation. My in-law's quiet home had just been invaded by us with two energetic little boys in tow. Always the perfect hostess, Jean had our rooms ready and a refrigerator stocked full of our favorite items. As Saturday rolled around, Jean needed a well-deserved nap. She asked if I would please unload the clothes from the washer into the dryer when the cycle ended. "Of course!", I said. However, just a few short minutes later I decided to go shopping quickly forgetting the "little thing" asked of me. My favorite store was in Marty's hometown of Murfreesboro and I kept the credit card paid off for trips home just like this one. I returned before Jean woke up, but thought nothing more about the wash. After all, at this stage of my life I often left the clothes in the washer for hours, if not days. No big deal, right? Wrong! Jean awoke to the family gathered talking excitedly and making a mess in her kitchen. She smiled and greeted everyone as she walked to the laundry room. Martin had the misfortune of walking by at the same time Jean realized the wash had not been moved. That woman was mad! I had never seen or heard her angry before and I shrank into myself. I overheard her words declaring all she had done to prepare this house and I could not even do one little thing like move the laundry. Ashamed of myself, I ran into hiding and never apologized or spoke of it again, nor did she.

I look back at my young self and wonder who I was. Remember, "little things matter"? What harm an issue like that could have become. Perhaps, it could even have driven a wedge between us had Jean held a grudge. Her amnesty helped me learn quick forgiveness and/or a sincere apology terminates the bitter seed eager to grow with just a few drops of water from the well of "unsaid words". It took work and patience to love me through my, oh so many, "so-'n-so" deeds.

I often stood amazed at her flowery graciousness after I had tromped through her forgiveness garden unaware. Her choice to pull out shoots of bitterness that had sprung up before they took root, allowed room for pardon and an example of grace as I plodded along through my "all about me" years.

It *is* all about us, though. Oh yes, we live our lives as if our fellow man is important to us, but just wait until our preferences are challenged. Not you, you say? Tell me about the type of worship service you attend. Many of us stand firm that we would not be caught dead in a service with drums while others say a service without clapping and the raising of hands is already dead.

A few years ago, one of the missionaries from our church shared a story of three women who had in recent years become followers of Christ, in their three separate locations. To profess faith in Jesus could have devastating results in their countries so, secretly, all three women lived their new Christian lives longing for godly fellowship through worship. One Easter, the missionary was able to get the three women from their various cities together to worship as a congregation of three. Their longings were replaced with great joy as they praised God with others for the first time. They sang with such appreciation for His kindness.

> *"I will tell of Thy name to my brethren; in the midst of the assembly I will praise Thee."*
> Psalm 22:22

This report stopped me in my tracks. Just a few minutes earlier, I had mentally critiqued our worship service thinking how weary I was of singing one of the songs, again. Shame on me! Worship is about God and not about me and my desires. The missionary's story struck accord. I had just been a "so-'n-so" to the Lord.

When the prophet Isaiah saw a vision of the Lord before him, he responded,

> *"Woe is me, for I am ruined! Because I am a man of unclean lips, and I live among a*

*people of unclean lips; for my eyes have seen
the King, the Lord of hosts."* Isaiah 6:5

In the previous chapters, Isaiah had been laughed
at and ignored by the people he was sent to warn. The
treatment he received from these people was not fair.
It was *their* lives of apostasy seen by God and Isaiah
had urged them to turn from their evil ways and trust
Him. In quite a turn of events, Isaiah finds himself
now in the presence of the Lord. His first words
reflect the accurate view he had of himself *"I am a
man of unclean lips"*. He did not say, "those turkeys
who laughed at me are now going to get theirs." No,
he spoke first of his own sin and plight and *then* of
the sin of the people God had called him to warn.
How often I fail to take the log out of my own eye
before attempting to show others the speck in theirs?
But we live in a world of self, claiming our rights as
we quicken our steps to criticize when those rights
are threatened.

How do you respond to a "so-'n-so"? Does
it seem they are all around you? Could *you* be the
common denominator? Don't we even revel in being
a "so-'n-so" sometimes? We may claim it as a right.
Subsequently, a self-righteous attitude unleashes a
Dr. Jekell-like side, sabotaging our mask of control.
Usually, a desperate need sparks this action. The
attention we crave becomes masqueraded in a
disturbing package, breeding misery. This misery
germ is catching and spreads quickly to the innocent.
Defensive emotions respond and retaliatory remarks
ensue as a "so-'n-so" flu is born.

Long before Jean and I shared the platform to speak on "in-law relationships", we agreed that *everybody* can be a "so 'n so", just like her friend had said. We saw that resolution lined up with Scripture.

*"The heart is more deceitful than all else and is desperately sick; Who can understand it?"* Jeremiah 17:9

*"For all have sinned; fall short of the glory of God."* Romans 3:23

We determined since we all have the same deceitful heart, we are all guilty. Which means you, me and even the compassionate Jean Moseley, can be a "so-'n-so".

# Lesson 3

# *This Too Shall Pass*

We're all "so-'n-sos" more often then we want to admit. I recall telling Jean about grabbing that title again as I conversed with a new acquaintance at our church. The conversation had been so pleasant and yet I made a few comments in an effort to promote myself to this new friend. Ashamed, I asked Jean if I would ever learn. "Sweetie", she had said, "this too shall pass. You will still make mistakes like this but with a little work and self examination; you will make them less and less as your wisdom grows.

> *"Behold, Thou dost desire truth in the innermost being, and in the hidden part Thou wilt make me know wisdom."* Psalm 51:6

My wisdom often waned in the hurriedness of my schedule as a young mom. I thought the more I was doing at church, the kids' school and at home meant I was successful as a mother, wife and friend. I had three calendars going so I could keep the plates spinning. The mistakes I made I justified as a by-product of the uncontrollable demands on my life. Jean loved to ask me a question after an especially stressful list of issues I had dealt with for the day: *"Besides that, Mrs. Lincoln, how was the play?"* It always made me laugh, but it also helped put things in perspective. Unlike Mrs. Lincoln, my husband had not just been shot. I was just busy. Everybody had schedules, everybody had stresses and I wasn't the first to have a lot going on. Jean reminded me the truth that this time of my life will never come again. Try to focus on today because tomorrow is only a few hours away and this moment will be gone. I needed an attitude adjustment to change my outlook, in good times and bad, enough to notice who was around me rather than simply running past the world in my hurry.

But how about your in-law? You've heard the saying, *"You can't change anyone else, but you can change yourself."* Yeah, yeah, we've all heard it. But we knew there was something missing in that statement. We are not the changers. Only the work of the Holy Spirit can reconstruct our ways convicting and convincing a heart to change. We are to

> *"put on the new self, which in the likeness of God has been created in righteousness and holiness of the truth."* Ephesians 4:24

40

Our attitudes, even with the best of efforts in communication, can still show themselves as self-serving to those that can't quite see where we are coming from. Our communication is sometimes flawed.

When our oldest son was eagerly awaiting his third birthday, he instructed me with these words, *"Don't you bollalow, I bollalow!"* I looked at him dumbfounded and tried to understand what he had said. He repeated it so many times he became frustrated and angry. The last thing I wanted to do at that point was *bollalow* anything, but I was now dealing with a misunderstood crazed three year old.

Hours later, after his tears and tantrums led him to time in the corner, I asked the Lord to help me figure out how to "clue into" this child. We spoke different languages. It wasn't until his birthday rolled around and he stood over his cake did I realize what he had been pleading about. You see on his second birthday we had helped him blow out the candles on the cake. This year he was asking us not to bollalow, blow out, the candles but to let him do it himself.

Just as it took effort to learn what my son was trying to say in his limited ability, we must learn the language of our in-laws to understand what they are trying to convey by their actions. In the midst of their "so-'n-so" ness, we become as dysfunctional as they are by expressing negative responses. We fear this part of our lives *"never shall pass"*.

I discovered four biblical steps to assist toward freeing oneself of these hindrances as I studied various passages of Scripture. God's word shows us the value of opening the door for the Holy Spirit to use His word to help us be who He wants us to be. God's word to us doesn't give an option whether to love one another, our neighbors or our enemies. It's a command. If we take some steps to allow His work in us, that rogue in-law just may see a difference in you and come around. What is there to lose? There just may be a lot to gain like the joyful knowledge your Lord is smiling and saying, *"That's My girl!"*

Let's begin our steps keeping in mind the following Ephesians passage of a calling, an action plan and a purpose…

> *"…walk in a manner worthy of the calling with which you have been called, with all humility and gentleness, with patience, showing forbearance to one another in love, being diligent to preserve the unity of the Spirit, in the bond of peace."* Ephesians 4:1b-2

The *calling* is to walk in a worthy manner because your sovereign God is the One who has called you; the *action plan* is to do so with humility, gentleness, patience and forbearance; and the *purpose* is to love one another, allow unity of the Spirit and be bound in peace. Four steps can help you to walk into God's action plan.

## Step One: Get an accurate view of yourself.

Ephesians tells us to walk in a manner worthy of our calling as Christians. This walk starts with humility. A humble manner is how we get that accurate view of ourselves. This concept of accuracy rings true for me when I apply make-up to my 50+ year old face. In the last few years, I have found the need to use a magnifying mirror more and more in the application process. I examine myself closely and boy is it humbling. I see all of my imperfections and the many areas concealer is needed. I heard a pastor once say, "If the barn needs paintin', then paint it!" Oh, that mirror showed paint was in order. I would only be fooling myself if I chose to use a compact mirror for daily "paintin".

This notion is the same in my spiritual walk. Do I view my actions from afar and others with a magnifying glass? What would be revealed if I turned that mirror around and got a good look at myself?

In checking ourselves, our motives and our humbleness, we can see how the "action plan" comes into play by walking our calling with patience and gentleness. We can't be patient or gentle alone. We have to practice it on others. We are even told to do so with "forbearance" which means to "put up with", resulting in the unity of the Spirit and the bond of peace…God's plan.

If that "so-'n-so" germ is lurking within you, maybe some needful time before the Lord's magnified mirror can reflect where humility is needed and the "*former manner of life is laid aside.*" Ephesians 4:22a

In His presence our flaws lie exposed. Two doors stand before us as we gaze in God's mirror and a choice must be made. Do we choose the door of self rule or the door granting God's control and our humility? The humility door allows a renewed spirit of mind as He brings light to hallways leading toward gentleness, kindness and hope of reconciliation. While the door of self rule continues in the "*old self being corrupted in accordance with the lusts of deceit.*" Ephesians 4:22b-23

We must get an accurate view of ourselves.

### Step Two: Watch what comes out of your mouth.

The book of James tells us how destructive our words can be:

> "*With it* [tongue] *we bless our Lord and Father; and with it we curse men, who have been made in the likeness of God...Does a fountain send out from the same opening both fresh and bitter water?*" James 3:9, 11 [bracket added by me]

I lived this out one Sunday as my husband and I were on the 20 mile drive home after church debriefing about the morning's service. As one of the worship leaders, he was especially joyful how the service had gone. I, on the other hand, had attended a meeting becoming disgruntled over a minor issue. In the midst of expressing my position to Marty he began to take up my offense becoming disgruntled, too. I had just come from "blessing" our Lord and now I was cursing another. Not only that, but I had pulled Marty from a fountain of joy into a stream of bitter water.

I remember as a child, adults would say, "You better watch your mouth!" That saying always cracked me up. The visual of trying to "watch your mouth" seemed as ridiculous as when my father would yell to my sister and me, as we bickered in the backseat of the car, *"Do you want me to come back there?"* We would giggle and quietly think, *"Yea, Dad, you are going 70 miles an hour down the highway. Come on back!"*

We can't physically see what our mouth is doing unless we stand in front of a mirror, but we are capable of putting our brains into action before the tongue lets loose.

I know what you are thinking. What about when someone is determined to get to you? Their fierce exercise shows the intention of looking for a fight. My mother used to say, *"If you are in the right, don't do anything to put yourself in the wrong."* Failure to heed this avenue of advice is common to fallen man and woman. Oh how we want to slam dunk our detractors with the truth of how incorrect they are. Jean would often counsel me to remain silent and let the person's words echo in their ears. Many a time she asked me if I had considered the shoes the offender may have walked in. It works! I have even felt sorrow for an accuser when their words do seem to come back to them. No, it did not justify their actions but it allowed me to see a hint of the grace I receive when I offer it to others. It is hard to keep my self-righteous feeling of injustice when I view someone's anger shift to regret. The mouth *does* get us into trouble, for from it flow the issues of the heart. (Proverbs 4:23)

My uncontrolled tongue used to put me in danger daily. During our Colorado years, I co-led our women's ministries with another woman. It was a big position and I was far from qualified, but hid it well. One day, I fumed to my friend, Lois, about the mistakes and inadequacies of many of our women. Lois took a deep breath and said, "Gee, Mimi, it sure seems like everyone had a struggle today." I stood convicted as the issues of my heart were revealed and flowed forth. Criticizing others was a symptom of my condition. I had not guarded my heart diligently, hence moving God off the throne and seating myself down. What poured from my lips was a testimony to my spiritual walk. I had not watched the path of my feet nor kept my eyes fixed ahead. (Proverbs 4:25-26)

Abraham Lincoln once said, "Better to remain silent and be thought a fool than to speak out and remove all doubt."

The two steps of getting an accurate view of myself and watching what comes out of my mouth accomplished a lot, but more steps were needed.

## Step Three: Pray, then act!

*"And I say to you, ask, and it shall be given to you; seek, and you shall find; knock, and it shall be opened to you...Now suppose one of you fathers is asked by his son for a fish; he will not give him a snake instead of a fish, will he?...If you then, being evil, know how to give good gifts to your children, how much more shall your heavenly Father give the Holy Spirit to those who ask Him?"* Luke 11:9, 11, 13

Jesus was telling His disciples there would be opposition and they needed to pray. He also beseeched them to seek His help and not to give up. Keep knocking, keep asking Him for help. When your in-law is driving you nuts, step away from the ledge and go to God in prayer for her! Ask Him what to do, then do it! He put her in your life and He is the only One who can give you strength and wisdom to show grace, gentleness or construct a boundary if necessary.

I confess I have occasionally prayed the Lord would open the earth and swallow my offender. If you have felt that way, too, pray anyway. He has a way of taking our honesty and speaking truth to our most inner places. Our prayers open the way for the Lord to work in our heart. Over time, the Holy Spirit will grant a love thought impossible. It is the attitude He will change allowing peace to the soul. Be patient, He may allow a practice in humility to go on quite awhile before the first bud of hope with your in-law is seen. Or a change may never come, but a peace that passes all understanding will settle on you instead.

Trust there is a reason He allows it to take as long as it does. Remember when Martha called for Jesus when Lazarus was sick? Christ delayed for His purpose which was "*...that they may believe...*" (John 11:42) None would question whether Martha would have traded the results. No, I'm confident she celebrated when her brother was raised from the dead and so many came to the saving knowledge of Christ because of Jesus' delay.

Maybe the conflict with an in-law is as dead as Lazarus was. Friend, if Jesus can raise a man dead in the grave for four days, He can work a miracle in your life, so pray!

**Step Four: Seek wisdom**

*"The wise woman builds her house, but the foolish tears it down with her own hands."*
Proverbs 14:1

I've lived this verse a few hundred times. Through the many opportunities of tearing down, I discovered how I can think of the "*house*" in that verse as a barometer of my closeness to the Lord. My walk with Christ seems good. Check! Prayer life? Yep! Check! And what about the blessing of knowing the Lord was building His house within me? Check! But somewhere in doing His will, I begin to neglect my time with Him distracted by the pull to pursue my own way and do what is right in my eyes. Surprised, I see my "house" turn to shambles. I'm not very good at being God, but I find myself foolishly trying to take the role.

Asking for wisdom is a humbling task. The admission that things aren't working, as the mess intensifies, leaves us empty and now ready for Christ's filling. He takes our empty, weak shell and pours in His promise to teach us from each trial. Sure we want to take His role again, but we vie for it less and less. He wants to help us as He places desires in our hearts to draw us back. We moved, not Him. He's right there.

> *"Surely goodness and love will follow me all the days of my life and I will dwell in the house of the Lord forever."* Psalm 23:6 (NIV)

If *"goodness and love"* are following, they must be close. Perhaps we just need to stop, turn around, and receive. Wisdom must be sought. It can be found in the shape of a Sunday message from the pulpit, a hymn or praise chorus or may even come in the shape of a godly older woman.

Living so far away from Jean, I often had the need to reach out to someone closer to home for immediate face-to-face counsel. I am happy to say I have known plenty of older women ready to listen and help me find the way to live and tell me where to turn. These women have walked their faith for years and have valuable experiences, especially placed in their lives, for them to encourage others.

> *"Blessed be the God and Father of our Lord Jesus Christ, the Father of mercies and God of all comfort; who comforts us in all our afflic- tion so that we may be able to comfort those who are in any affliction with the comfort with which we ourselves are comforted by God."*
> II Corinthians 1:3-4

Some women have stumbled and hit mistake- filled potholes along their roads or others have helped to pick friends up out of the mire along the way. There are women who have seen children and husbands die unexpectedly; marriages saved and some fail; as well as seen the joy of a life lived according to God's plan. What a wealth of resources are waiting to help as we walk our roads. Watch them! You will see the ones who have learned these four steps and more. They have learned to humbly check their hearts by allowing the Lord to help them get an accurate view of them- selves. Many have learned the hard way to watch what comes out of their mouths. And I can guarantee they have learned to pray and seek wisdom. They are eager to tell their stories of how God worked in their pain and how *this too shall pass.*

## Lesson 4

# *Build Bridges*

J ean was an educator, but also constructed bridges in her spare time. Not the Brooklyn or Golden Gate variety but bridges none the less that firmly connected vast divides between people. Teaching junior high students offered many occasions to work on her bridges. Some teachers would run screaming into the streets if given the assignment of junior high students, yet Jean embraced them, constantly looking for new ways to get through and build not only into the students' lives, but also into those same teachers running away.

As the problem attitudes of some children made themselves known, she saw her need to draw a design for this bridge building. Beginning with support beams she used significant moments to create the needed bridge for those kids to cross. Unfortunately, even with a secure bridge available to take the students places they never thought they could possibly go, many chose to sit on the shore of complacency. Aside from those on the shore, a few looked into Jean's sweet eyes and believed her bridge led to a better way.

Her thrill at those occasional responses kept her building regardless who crossed. Jean chose to listen to the cries of those young people's hearts in their rebellion, fighting, poor grades or the silent wail as they slept through class. She knew they struggled to hide extreme personal and family pain while feeling betrayed by a body lost between childhood and teenage years. The misery some of those children saw in their homes weighed on them constantly. They purposefully avoided sleep in case the fears of the home escalated during the night, and yet not knowing how to respond if disaster struck.

Some boys and girls had hard exteriors Jean never could crack. They treated other students and teachers with malice and never seemed remorseful for their actions. She felt a special love for those not fortunate enough to be born into her family. They were Jean's charges and part of her calling. They did not deserve her kindness or patience, but receive it they did. The Lord used Jean as His willing tool. After all, the hammer does not tell the carpenter where to strike.

Thankfully, not all of Jean's students experienced such anger or fears. But she realized each child faced some area of need and it was important to give them life lessons as they reached for rays of hope. Jean refused to let them go until she had expended her best effort to love and teach them. Praying for wisdom, she went a little further to instill discipline while seeking to understand the pain lying just beneath the surface.

Many years of teaching granted Jean the respected position as *mentor teacher*. Even in this position, times began to change and the new age of "younger is better" emerged. She saw favoritism shown to younger teachers year after year. She watched, yet never complained, allowing the truth to speak for itself. She chose to teach as if each of her classes were at the top and was rewarded with students achieving goals beyond anyone's expectations.

The younger teachers watched Jean's example of calm acceptance and at times even attempted to take up an offense on her behalf. Well aware of the snubbing she received, they noted, not a word left her mouth. They learned in hindsight she had been building a bridge of character for them to cross one day.

### The Bridge Builder

An old man, going a lone highway,
came, at the evening, cold and gray,
to a chasm, vast, and deep, and wide,
through which was flowing a sullen tide.

The old man crossed in the twilight dim;
The sullen stream had no fears for him;
But he turned, when safe on the other side,
And built a bridge to span the tide.

"Old man," said a fellow pilgrim, near,
"You are wasting strength with building here;
Your journey will end with the ending day;
You never again must pass this way;
You have crossed the chasm, deep and wide-
Why build you a bridge at the eventide?"

The builder lifted his old gray head:
"Good friend, in the path I have come," he said,
"There followeth after me today,
A youth, whose feet must pass this way.

This chasm, that has been naught to me,
To that fair-haired youth may a pitfall be.
He, too, must cross in the twilight dim;
Good friend, I am building the bridge for him."

Author: Will Allen Dromgoole

Public Domain

What a vivid example this poem is of what
Jean did for these teachers. Each saw wisdom and
servant-hood modeled. She indeed built the bridge,
stone by stone so those behind her could cross with
the empowerment to build bridges of their own.

Isn't that an equally good example of what
mothers-in-law could do for their son's wife? We
who have been daughters-in-law already know it's
not easy. Maybe we have met with some less than
cordial in-laws and can begin building a bridge for
the girls who come behind us.

Jean used this bridge illustration in every interaction with women, not just me. A few months after her death, I met with those young teachers for whom she modeled bridge construction. Jean called them "the girls". Margaret Moore, Sheila Bratton and Elizabeth Church are three women I envy because of the close, unique relationship they had shared with my mother-in-law. These three lucky gals saw Jean day-in and day-out under pressure, through rejection and frustration, as well as little victories along her way that broke down barriers in students' lives and built up her own identity of integrity. Oh how I desired to know Jean that way, too. Listening to "the girls" reminisces about Jean, I wanted to squeeze every drop of her out of them and keep it for myself. But no, this special set of relationships was tailor made by the Lord to encourage them! I sat transfixed as they told their stories. Jean's quality was reflected in each woman. I heard her sayings and saw her mannerisms as if she were standing in our midst. I sat content to be in their company and thanked God for my own unique relationship as Jean's daughter-in-law.

Standing at the mirror of the restroom after our meeting, I looked and asked myself, "Will Jean be reproduced as powerfully in me as in these women? Will my daughters-in-law grasp the wonder of this woman as they watch me model Jean's influence to them?" I desperately want to say and pour so much into my girls, but I fail so often. It seems I step over boundaries and often become a "so 'n so". I have their best interest in mind but often speak first and listen later. The mirror reflected more than I wanted

to see. Tears returned to my eyes as I remembered
words from my Personal Trainer's manual,

*"...But let everyone be quick to hear, slow to
speak and slow to anger;"* James 1:19

*"Trust in the Lord with all your heart, and
do not lean on your own understanding."*
Proverbs 3:5

I sighed, surrendered again and prayed not only
that Anna and Rebecca would see Jean's qualities in
me, but above all, they would see the One Jean and I
serve, Jesus. Jean would be quick at a time like this
to make me smile with a great line such as *"some
mistakes are too much fun to just do once."*

How fortunate my daughters-in-law manage
to find humor in my interference and are quick to
forgive. I especially miss Jean when the times come
to impart wisdom to these young, blossoming wives.
Jean would know what to say and tell me when to
keep my mouth closed. The urge to reach out to her
reminded me of all the loving lessons she had taught
me. I cried out to the Lord instead. Jean's example of
seeking Christ did weave its way into my resolve to
build bridges. I couldn't do this on my own. I needed
to beseech the Lord's help to love these girls by first
asking His influence over my will before directing
me to action.

If my actions line up with His will, I will build
those bridges for my daughters-in-law and one day
they can choose to cross.

## Lesson 5

# *Seek Assistance Along Your Road*

Traveling the highways through "in-law" country, we see roads filled with plenty of "so-'n-sos" as well as some who seem a perfect fit for our style. Knowing we'll encounter various sojourners can be expected for those who've traveled the in-law road a long time. Just as predictable as driving the streets of our towns, we deal with the short-tempered drivers ready to honk as well as the gracious ones eager to allow us in front of them in heavy traffic. Regardless of the beauty of our way, a "so-n-so" can pull our attention from contentment to distraction by a blast of their horn.

As a young driver in Atlanta, I remember taking certain roads just to escape from the noise and congestion for a few moments of peace on beautiful little detours. My favorite one was called "The By Way". What a great name. This road had little to offer other than trees, but it provided a peaceful short cut after a day of stress. Sometimes when I need a day dream escape, I think back to those peaceful times on that road. This short ¾ mile stretch has not changed much over the years and on just about every trip back to Atlanta I make a point to drive out of my way to "The By Way".

You may remember some peaceful roads too, but typically we do not relate in-law relationships to peaceful roads. In fact, most folks would compare them to a traffic jam, a bridge out or a dead end.

Let's look at what we have on the roads. There are all kinds of vehicles: cars, trucks, motorcycles and buses. Some cars are blue, some are red, some are old and some are new…Before I break into a Dr. Seuss poem I'll get to the point. Though they are different and used in a variety of ways, they are still all cars. In the same way it is helpful to concentrate on our similarities in regards to our in-laws. We are all human. We all have joys and we have all experienced pain. Just because I have been on my road as a wife longer than my sons' wives does not make them any less wives. My bigger bumper, dinged doors and higher odometer just give evidence to what the chassis has endured along my journey.

In an effort to be a good mother-in-law, I attempt to show where the warning signs are which I have found through experiences along my road. Those who have helped me gain knowledge by pointing those signs out have afforded me a safer journey when I abide. But just like any drivers, it will be my girls' choice whether to heed warning signs set before them.

Don't some in-laws seem determined to run us off those roads as they plow through caution markers? Haven't we all passed people, or had them pass us at a high rate of speed, wondering what can possibly be going on in their heads to make them drive the way they do. Does the term "idiot" come to mind? We assume a wild driver must be crazy. Have you ever done something "crazy" on the road? I sure have. I can remember impatiently driving my boys somewhere and being delayed as I caught every light and feeling it must be every driver's job to make me even later. I used my horn a few times and floored the accelerator in an effort to get to our destination faster. I can still see one of my son's with white knuckled hands on the dash board turn to me pleading, *"Mom, it's okay if I'm late. Please slow down!"* Tears still come to my eyes when I remember how dangerous it was and what the result could have been. I *was* crazy and a bit of an idiot, I admit.

What about the other dangerous drivers? The ones who honk, swerve over in your lane or sit on your bumper? Are they all *really* crazy? My husband says yes. Maybe, but if we pulled each one over to the side of the road and asked them, we might find more going on than the irritatingly obvious. As the mother of a diabetic child, I often pushed the limits to rush to his school when a major insulin reaction occurred. We think we have control and just this once I have cause to drive extreme.

Perhaps desperation pushed a typically safe driver into the "crazy" category. Maybe he just got fired or her spouse just announced he wants out of the marriage. Of course, it is not wise to get behind a wheel when we are emotionally charged, but many of us do. We don't know what others on the road are going through, yet oddly, we feel justified to judge them. A stressed driver can be defused by letting them out into traffic ahead of us. What does it cost us? Nothing! What does it grant that person? A break!

Dealing with in-laws can be the same way. Sometimes we need to offer some graciousness in the form of a little break to our in-law in desperation. Those of us who have traveled the in-law road longer know what a blessing an extra measure of understanding can be to the less traveled. Unfortunately, we do not come with neon lights over our heads warning us of the road conditions going on inside them. Wouldn't it be great to have one of those yellow informational signs pop up in the nick of time to divert us from driving into trouble?

One of the roads encountered might have a sign declaring "Icy road ahead!" There you are in your daily travels and heading toward a meeting with an in-law. You are aware of "inclement weather" in your relationship, yet caught off-guard as inno-cent comments send you slip-sliding down the icy highway of in-law winter. Once the spinning stops you are thankful you did not hit anyone or anything, but surprised at the fact you are facing in the wrong direction and stuck. How did you get there? What was your mistake? Why was the road in that condition anyway? With a little foresight, preventive measures could be made to keep the emotional car under control on those icy roads. God's Word tells us salt is good for icy conditions.

*"Let your speech always be with grace, seasoned, as it were, with salt, so that you may know how you should respond to each person."* Colossians 4:6

How many icy in-law winters could be thawed with the seasoning of God showing us how to respond? Unique "chain" restraints are in order to avoid in-law spinouts and other unfortunate accidents from happening. We need patience for the front tires and endurance for the back two when facing the cold, often unforgiving, elements of in-laws. Patience is defined in *Roget's New Millennium Thesaurus* - forgiving, gentle, long-suffering, quiet, understanding and untiring. Patience is my worst trait. I'm pretty quick to forgive, but the qualities of being quiet and untiring are daily struggles for me. When my boys were in school, I often said to myself, "I spend my entire life *waiting* on someone." I wanted them to come out the door after school immediately and quickly became agitated when all other students happily jumped in their parents cars while I again waited. Regardless of the reason for their delay, my mood had changed. These poor kids had legitimate reasons for not bounding out so I had to adjust my impatience to understanding. It did not come naturally.

Endurance is defined = abide, allow, experience lived through, or undergone. Sounds like Someone I know. Oh, how we plead with Christ to make us more like Him when we are on gentle roads like the "The By-Way," where the road is lovely and peaceful. By answering our plea, Christ in His infinite wisdom may send us down an icy in-law road to refine us in practicing caution, discipline and self-control. We cry out to Him for understanding after plowing into unexpected snow banks of in-law difficulty leaving us shivering in the cold.

Patience and endurance are each attributes of Jesus. We expect Him to be patient with us and give us plenty of warnings before He allows a consequence. He endured so much in His death for our sakes. He continued to abide with the Father though ridicule and rejection were all around Him. Can we not endure the life set before us?

Could we have avoided this most recent icy patch had we been more prepared with patience and endurance? I venture to say, "Yes!" with a disclaimer: To know the in-law road you travel you must study the route. Get to know your in-law. What makes her tick? What ticks her off? Become a student of her "map" and ask the Lord for His AAA roadside assistance as you travel. In God's AAA service, the A's stand for *Accept, Acknowledge* and *Affirm.*

- <u>Accept</u> – We are drawn with an everlasting love by the Lord and are told to love one another, love our neighbors and oh yes, love our enemies.

*"But I say to you, love your enemies, and pray for those who persecute you."* Matthew 5:44

- Acknowledge – We don't know what we don't know. God's ways and reasons for having you and me where we are is His deal. Asking for understanding enables us to walk on the path He has laid before us.

*"Give me understanding, that I may observe Thy law, and keep it with all my heart. Make me walk in the path of Thy commandments, for I delight in it."* Psalm 119:34-35

- Affirm – We all appreciate encouragement and most of us relish the opportunity to grant it. We have the power and obligation to give credit when it is due.

*"Do not withhold good from those to whom it is due, when it is in your power to do it."* Proverbs 3:27

Those icy roads are a mess without roadside assistance. Calling on this AAA and studying your in-law's "map" can reveal where the potholes and other trouble spots are located. Once the road is clear and your AAA Guide is directing, you gain the joy of viewing a terrain otherwise missed along the way. Fear can cause us to avoid the trip and overlook the beauty of the experience found on those icy roads.

I think that may be one of the reasons God put Titus 2:3-5 in the Bible:

*"Guide older women into lives of reverence so they end up as neither gossips nor drunks, but models of goodness. By looking at them, the younger women will know how to love their husbands and children, be virtuous and pure, keep a good house, be good wives. We don't want anyone looking down on God's Message because of their behavior."* Titus 2:3-5 (The Message)

It seems logical that those of us on our in-law roads longer would be the best examples, and many are, but why don't we see more of them making an effort toward the younger women? Be assured older women, the young gals are watching you. Just as you observe and possibly judge how the younger live, they take note to see if you are the kind of older woman they want to emulate. Are the words of your mouth and the meditations of your heart acceptable to the Lord and exemplary to others? (Psalm 19:14) Sure this younger group of contemporaries may seem self-sufficient and capable, but many a young heart is screaming for direction signs on her road. Don't you want your daughter-in-law to have success with her family? Of course you do, but you may need some salt on your road to keep her from sliding into a ditch.

Many of these gals have experienced poor examples in their own mothers and seen terrible examples of unhealthy marriages. They are determined to see why some marriages make it while others fail. They are hungry to hear success stories and even mistakes so they can work toward healthy marriages and families. But just like you, they have to work it out in their lives. You may be giving the best counsel possible only to have it rejected. Give her time and love her as you stand close by.

How does a new wife today learn to care for her husband and family without the influence of mature women? The Titus two passage ends with a caution:

*"We don't want anyone looking down on God's Message because of their behavior."* (The Message)

We have all heard folks say, "If that's what it looks like to be a Christian, count me out!" Our actions speak louder than words when we choose to be either good examples or bad ones as we represent God to our daughters-in-law. Remember, our actions as followers of Christ may be the only Bible some people ever read.

Does your daughter-in-law seem to be making mistakes? It's hard to understand this younger generation sometimes. They are just not doing things the way you did as a young Christian woman. You may even see these gals doing just fine without your help, so you choose *not* to step forward believing there is nothing left to offer and assuming they wouldn't want it even if you did. Investigate your daughter-in-law. Look for her making positive steps and affirm her along her road.

Yet I employ you, listen to them and you will hear they are very aware of their need for more seasoned women in their lives. Maybe a little time with some of the younger women of your church will help you understand your daughter-in-law. It's a different culture today, but our calling as Titus two women remains the same. You may discover some of these young ladies have felt the rejection of a spouse's mother and crave your influence and experience.

After questioning mothers-in-law, it's now the daughters-in-law turn. Many of you might very well be better educated and more savvy in this world, but there is so much you don't know due to lack of life experiences. Give some credit to your husband's mother. The world is a different place than when your mother-in-law was a young wife. You may unknowingly be giving the impression you have a handle on it all leaving her to feel she has nothing to offer.

In my years of ministering to women, more and more of you say your mothers have been too busy with their lives and careers to teach you the basics: to cook, clean or raise a family. Sure you can bring home the bacon, fry it up in a pan and never let your husband forget he's a man, but you still feel you fall short. You are quick to ask other young women what to do when little Ethan won't eat his dinner or nap but find these same gals have no more experience than you do. You are intimidated by your mother-in-law so you choose not to call her. Take a chance and ask her questions about her son. And when your mother-in-law gives you good advice, tell her and thank her for it. Find ways to encourage. God is still at work and very aware you both grew up on different roads and in different cultures. Watch for Him to work and savor the love lessons as He teaches you. Leave the needed changes to God.

After a women's retreat, I asked one of our older ladies, Doris, who was known as a great cook to teach a cooking class for the younger women. She was thrilled as she prepared the menu and all the "fixins." (Southern, for ingredients.) The day of the class we squeezed 35 women into our little church kitchen. Each young gal sat eagerly listening to the recipe directions laced with wisdom from this Titus two woman. She would pause to tell the women little nuggets like, "Girls, when your husband comes home don't hit him with the events of the day. Give him a plate of cheese and crackers on the bedroom table and let him unwind a little. He will come back out more prepared to listen and play with the children." The girls' mouths dropped open. It seemed like common sense but the idea was revolutionary to them. Doris set lovely signs up along her road that were seen and followed by many. To this day, she is a favorite of the younger women and many in-betweeners, like me.

If the discouragement of the relationship with your mother-in-law is extreme, pray God will bring a mature woman to offer counsel and pray with you. You can't pick your mother-in-law, but you surely can seek out a woman who shows a love and accep-tance because of the love and acceptance Jesus has shown her. Look around your church. These women are there and ready to encourage you in your calling to be kind and gentle, to love your family and teach what is good so that *"the word of God is not dishonored."*

During a recent trip to work with an urban missions group in New Orleans I learned how narrow my road of understanding and acceptance was. We visited "the projects" to paint a family's apartment. We had been told the 15-year-old daughter, who had just given birth to a baby, had accepted Christ and was beginning growth along her road. Painting and observing the interaction and patterns of this family of nine sharing a two bedroom apartment, and especially viewing this young mother, I determined there was no evidence of Christ in that home. It was roach infested and I could not even imagine how they ate in the kitchen much less cleaned themselves in the bathroom. When we gathered back at the missions office, we learned how the young mother and her brother were growing in their faith. I held my tongue as the director spoke of these two young people. I wondered if she was easily misled or if she just wanted desperately for their budding faith to be true.

Right smack in the middle of her words I felt the Lord challenge my heart. It was as if He said, "Who are you to evaluate how I am working in this place? The way I work is different in this culture than your middle class church environment in California!" I was judging by what I thought knew, but the Lord was trying to teach me to understand Him better by loving and accepting without judgment. Could He be saying the same to you?

*"Do not judge lest you be judged. For in the way you judge, you will be judged; and by your standard of measure, it will be measured to you."* Matthew 7:1-2

Just as we are to be cautious about judging, we are also to acknowledge the things they do well and affirm them. We do not have permission to withhold encouragement because we are too focused on all we disagree with.

Years ago, I had a wonderful woman mentor me. She was quite a bit older and gave me so many great tools as a leader and speaker. But in all the times we met, she never affirmed me when I had accomplished the tasks given. Instead, she critiqued the many ways I fell short. I began to wonder if I would ever improve. The lack of appropriate affirmation can, and eventually will, discourage and leave us ineffective. When we seek wisdom, the Lord grants it. When we care for His people He does not withhold His pleasure and neither should we.

One woman who was quick to encourage the younger women was Dorothy. This older woman in our church made the intentional decision to reach out to the younger women. This choice required a sacrifice. Dorothy loved our traditional worship service with its liturgy and old hymns, but when a Sunday school class opened up for the 20-30 year olds and needed an older couple to be available in the class, she prayed then dragged her husband to the class. She gave up her preferred service. Dorothy met so many of the younger gals and loved hearing of their interests and was amazed to see they cherished the encouragement she offered from her life experiences.

By joining this class, Dorothy's only church service option was to attend the more contemporary worship all the young people attended. She smiled as the choruses and drums were played and even clapped her hands. She later told me she would not have traded the blessing of meeting these girls for all the traditional services in the world. She learned aspects of this younger culture and was an invaluable asset to them. It also helped her in relating to her children, their spouses and grandchildren. She made a sacrificial choice that granted her the unique opportunity to offer help to others along the road.

What's on your road? It may be flat and well paved or hilly and full of potholes. Even on good roads obstacles appear out of nowhere and block your way. Things you did not ask for or deserve. Yet, there it stands. You may be called to hack a path in the forest of dismal results where all of your efforts may fall on deaf ears. Will you feel alone and desperate? Jesus knows. He has placed you where you are because He wants to use YOU to reach that woman. Were Jean alive today she would tell you her efforts with me were worth it. Partly because she saw my tough exterior soften over the years, but mainly because God was faithful to hear her when she called. So faithful, she could look back over her life without regrets.

Of course there are life-long in-law situations that may never improve. Some of you reading may even feel a sense of regret for a relationship where death came before reconciliation occurred. No way to fix it now, so regret hangs heavily overhead. Good news! You can change the condition of your road from here. Keep in mind the different generational cultures and strive to learn what contributes to the way your in-law thinks. God may be calling you to clear and pave a new road that was once blocked or even build a bridge. Go on! Build a bridge for others now that you have crossed the valley to the other side. Choose each day to love. Look for ways to help others love you. Drive your road carefully since you just may be the "so 'n so" in someone's life and only you can change that.

## Lesson 6

# *When You Build a Fence, Leave a Gate*

My son, Marty (yes, the same name as my husband) and his bride, Rebecca, rented a condo for their first home. It had everything a young couple needed and more, with two bedrooms, a washer and dryer, fireplace and a small backyard. They were thrilled to start their new life together in this little home. The yard needed a lot of work so my husband and I drove down to help get it started. We came prepared with tools and plants ready to work an *extreme makeover*. There was only one problem… no gate to the yard. We had to haul dirt, plants, and bricks through the house to the back, leaving a trail of our efforts on the carpet. We learned a gate entrance had not been added because home burglaries were common in the area and gate-free fencing was a deterrent. Effective against external invasion yes, conducive for internal improvement, no.

This gateless barrier illustrates what we might be building to protect our emotions by fencing the bad out of our lives. Is there a fence between you and your problem in-law? Do you find all attempts at kindness or gentleness fruitless? Have your efforts been returned with contempt and misunderstanding, leaving you more and more ready to give up?

Physical barriers are erected to pose as defensive mechanisms keeping unwanted people, animals, etc. out. Emotional barriers are built with anguished hands placing the indiscernible sign "Caution: Vulnerable Person Inside" on its wall. The sign is too small to see as visitors to the barrier walk around in confusion. In the midst of emotional pain, the fence keeps growing higher and thicker as the construction may resemble more of a fortress. Nothing gets in. I have to ask, does the offender see a healthy boundary has been set up or do they find a wall before them without a way in?

I built a tall significant wall years ago. This was not with an in-law, but the lesson in loving still applies. I worked in a support position for a woman I'll call Vicki. I wanted to be a good employee and friend to her. Instead of kindness, she seemed to gain pleasure in criticizing my faith and even calling me, "The Virgin Mary". This continued for months until finally I had had enough. In a fit of anger, I called Jean to complain. She told me, *"The person who angers you, controls you."* Whoa, that was it! Without considering anything more, I determined no longer to allow Vicki to have control over me. I settled in to build a wall between us so secure Army

Rangers could not break through. I would not engage her in any way except business matters from that day on. Is this starting to sound like your situation with your in-law?

As time progressed, Jean would ask me how things were going with Vicki and my reply was simple, "I went to work, did my job and came home."

"So, is it better between you two then?" Jean would ask.

Well, no it wasn't. I was indifferent to Vicki because I had yet to learn steps for walking in faith. I wanted *"this too shall pass"* to go on and pass. I refused to accept Vicki as a mission field, a cross to bear or one to love. In fact, with hindsight, I see my barrier had actually created a deeper resentment which fueled her fire. Vicki had felt intimidated by me from the day we met because I was a Christian and a close friend to our boss. My sudden disregard of her, granted out of self-protection, betrayed who I said I was and re-enforced her jaded view of Christians. She felt nothing but rejection and judgment from me. I had a window of opportunity to be a light, but I chose to close it and leave her in darkness. I made it all about me.

In time, Vicki left the company and I was thrilled. I was ready for life to improve, but it did not. My lack of respect for her had not only been evident to Vicki but to co-workers as well. Aware of her actions, they commented she was just that way and said I did not deserve her treatment. No one blamed me for my actions, but they saw that I had written her off. Many said it was exactly what *they* would have done, too.

Ouch! My wall had positioned me in the world and of it. I'd built a nice big barrier and fenced myself in.

Retelling this story still breaks my heart. I had made sure she would not hurt me again and cared nothing for any pain my actions caused. Vicki was not my in-law but she was a person, and the Lord in His sovereignty had placed her in my life for a purpose. Vicki *was* my mission field, my calling, the one I was to love. God intended me to build a bridge from Him to this lost one but I had erected an impenetrable barricade instead with a big "DO NOT ENTER" sign clearly posted. I made the choice to take things in my own hands keeping God blocked out as well. I built the perfect fence! Thick, secure and sealed tight.

Dr. Henry Cloud and Dr. John Townsend's book *"Boundaries"* discusses the need for *properly* placing limits so the boundary clearly states not only the reason for the separation, but a way for communication and even restoration to occur if the other person chooses to respect those boundaries.

Had I read their book during this time, I would have seen I had it all wrong. I had made my enclosure without informing Vicki. I assumed she knew she had offended me and I was inflicting the consequence. What a better result had I gone to Vicki in private and explained how I felt when she ridiculed my faith and called me embarrassing names. I could have asked her not to respond to me in such a way. At this point, conceivably, I would add if she did choose to continue to speak in this manner, I would not stand for it and a specific action would result. I would have made clear what action I would take and then follow through. Verbal, calm communication: what a concept! My way had erected a solid, gateless fence, offering no hope or opportunity for Vicki to break through.

Our fear of confrontation can leave us in a world of false perception. Issues with contentious family members can quickly catch us off guard when a rogue comment results in "opened mouth and inserted foot." Ideally, most families desperately want to love and live happily ever after. Sadly, when rejected or embarrassed their happy dream dies and so does the love. What should have been a blessed family now rivals *The Jerry Springer Show*.

Here is the heart of the question: In all honesty, do you even care? In-law issues can hurt so deeply you may believe only the other party is guilty, which may be the case. A rip in your heart can draw the curtain closed and hide reality. Your perception of innocence is so real you can't imagine any jury convicting you of wrong doing or misunderstanding. You would be deemed innocent by your testimony of self-defense.

Before the fence goes up, it is important to evaluate your level of responsibility for the problem. If your contribution is significant, own your part verbally to your in-law. She may have been building her own fence. If she is at fault, it is only fair to calmly tell her you set a boundary wall.

Many points of contention can be avoided by some pro-active planning. Jean started this process planting small hedges. She and I lived most of my married life on opposite ends of the country. When vacation times rolled around we tried to visit one family or the other. Finances were tight for us in those early years so Marty and I chose trips where we stayed for free. Martin and Jean's home in Murfreesboro, Tennessee topped our list. Family abounded and Jean always made us feel special. She opened her home as a retreat where we ate, slept and were entertained by family. Yes, they spoiled us.

One year we planned an unusually long stay in Murfreesboro. Our trip included all four of us for the first six days, and then Marty flew out for a conference as we stayed on four more days. I remember getting in the car to drive my husband to the airport and saying to Jean, *"One down, three to go!"* I saw a look of agreement on her face that spoke the truth of my statement. I thought about that look all the way to the Chattanooga Airport and back. It sparked a question I had wanted to ask for years.

Upon my return, I opened a stream of conversations about our visits to each other. I asked why she and Martin always stayed in hotels instead of our home. I assumed it was because our house was small. Jean wrote the following from her memory of how she answered that day.

> *"Some of the deepest hurts and worst feuds I've ever heard about came during holidays or vacations when several family units were together in a small place for several days. This is a fuss waiting to happen! We are so privileged in America to have elbow-*

*room, but when we suddenly lose our individual space, we become very testy. This is especially true when we set our sights too high: the perfect family Christmas or the perfect week at the beach where no one gets sunburned, tired, seasick or upset from eating too much food.*

*A shorter time together without being too close and we all still love each other in the end. Martin and I believe by staying in a hotel, you can have some time when you don't have to be "on" and we can have some time to rest and be quiet for a while."*

Jean validated me in her answer. It *was* wonderful, but draining when they visited. They stayed just long enough to love and laugh, but left before we grated on each other. Jean's candid response spoke the truth we both experienced. Cleaning, cooking and excursion planning is joyful, but not easy for either hostess. Their plan enabled us to absolutely love being together and made for terrific memory making.

Yes, we still went to visit in Murfreesboro *and* stayed in their home after learning their position, but we kept our visits to a few days and made a point to be out of the house for a while each day. They kept their schedules and meetings in place, giving them somewhere to escape as well. In an effort to guard consideration for each family, we communicated beforehand the activities we would be doing separately. It was a good system as we all enjoyed the freedom to come and go as we pleased.

Let me ask a few thought provoking questions. Do you expect your in-laws to entertain you when you visit? Do you expect them to put their lives on hold for you? What unspoken expectations are you foisting on them? Of course you have come to spend time with them and maybe spent a lot of money to do so. But here's a suggestion to shift the focus from being all about you. Before your visit, ask your in-law what commitments are set and what expectations they have of you. They may have their heart set on a family dinner every night when you want to go out. Consider a compliment to her cooking and how wonderful that sounds. Then ask if it would be okay if you took them to dinner one night to thank them for putting up with you on the trip. Also, offer to help set the table, clean up after dinner or strip the beds when you leave. Don't get your feelings hurt if she wants to clean the dishes herself. I never could load the dishwasher the way Jean liked and it frustrated her when I tried. She gave some non-verbal cues for me to back off, but finally had to tell me she preferred loading the dishes her way. I learned I could help her more if I cleared the table while she took care of the dishwasher.

Jean built her fence, not with brick and mortar, but lovingly created it to communicate and allow choices. Her boundary was a beautiful hedge with a welcome mat at the opening. A fence with a gate.

When Jean and I shared the stage for an in-law seminar, one attendee confronted Jean with a comment causing her to further explore the fence with an unreasonable in-law:

"The fence with a gate suggestion is great in a perfect world. I can see how ideally this would be helpful. My mother-in-law belittles me in front of my children. I need specific steps to take so I don't kill her."

This statement got Jean's attention. A Pollyanna answer would not suffice to this anguished young woman.

Jean took a deep breath and prayed before opening her mouth. She asked the Lord for wisdom and the ability to give His answer of hope.

"We have a choice," Jean said, "to be assertive or aggressive. The aggressive decision announces your feelings and desires without consideration for others. The assertive alternative proves the better choice and shows one is sensitive to the other, but not responsible for their actions."

"In the perfect world you mentioned, one would know when the next attack was coming and the mother-in-law would be receptive to the assertive approach. Unfortunately, we live in a fallen world and the hour to assert will come unexpectedly." She told the young woman, "Prepare for the inevitable and try to remain in control. Remember the one that angers you, controls you. When the offense occurs, ask the offender if she could help you with something in the other room. Once there, she will be ready for a fight. Stay quiet for a moment. Ask her to sit next to you. It is harder to fight sitting down. Pray quickly before you speak. Take a deep breath and speak her name softly."

*'The tongue of the wise makes knowledge acceptable..."* Proverbs 15:2a

Jean began a hypothetical scenario between Rita, the mother-in-law and the daughter-in-law, Shar. A harsh correction of Shar's parenting skills had just occurred in front of the children. After moving to another room Shar began gently:

*'Rita, I would like to share a concern about something with you. When situations like we just encountered arise, it's bad for everyone.' Shar's first step allows an opportunity for common ground. Unfortunately, that "common ground" will likely not be taken. Be prepared. An accusatory comeback is more probable. Let her go on until she takes a breath. If possible, gently touch her arm and say, 'This is what we need to discuss.' Do NOT let her remarks change your course.*

*Begin with a positive remark. Acknowledge her in some area in which she is successful. Perhaps there is a sacrifice she has made or a passion of hers you are thankful for. Carefully consider how "you" words are used. Strive to use a vocabulary that offers discussion in lieu of reprimand. More "I" and less "you" focused statements.*

*'Rita, I am so thankful when you come to visit. The children love you so much. I appreciate the time you make to drive over here since it is such a production for me to load up all the kids and come to you. I'd like your opinion on how concerned should we be when the children hear critical words between*

*their grandma and mommy? Neither of us would let them speak to us, or each other, that way, and yet it is what we portrayed today. Could you approach me away from their little ears? I know you've had much more experience than I and I welcome constructive ideas. I promise to listen and consider your advice. It's hard being a young mom and sometimes criticism makes me feel like a failure. Negative words keep me from hearing you. I become frustrated and respond in a way confusing to the kids. It's not good for anybody."*

With Jean's strategic plan, Shar affirmed and appreciated Rita first. Next, Shar gave common ground they could both agree on. Of course, a loving grandma does not want grandchildren to hear harsh words nor copy poor examples. Finally, Shar showed respect. She admitted her own experience was limited and that Rita indeed had valuable counsel. She simply asked Rita to present it differently.

Depending on Rita's response, Shar had to be ready with the assertiveness to close the gate, if need be. Caution! Do not take the route to close the gate too soon! You may need to repeat this process several times. Consider asking your in-law if she remembered your requests. Gently, remind her again. Only after concerted effort and patience do you inform her, the gate is closing. But be sure to help her see how to open the gate again.

Jean and I would admonish you to go back to the steps we discussed in Lesson 3's *"This Too Shall Pass"*.

1. Get an accurate view of yourself.
2. Watch what comes out of your mouth.
3. Pray, then act!
4. Seek wisdom.

Examine yourself to see what reality is. Perhaps you have been the offending in-law and some fences have been built to keep you out. Maybe you need to, or have had to, set some barriers yourself with in-laws. If so, have you left room for a gate of reconciliation?

After examining yourself, the next step asks us to *watch what comes out of our mouths*. Oh, there are times I have made one too many *suggestions* crossing a line with Rebecca or Anna only to be surprised with the gate of "interference" closed in my face. The girls are sweet to open the gate readily and offer me entrance which helps me to guard what comes out of my mouth more carefully.

Remember that third step is to PRAY? Hey, I'm not kidding. If you are not praying you will not be examining yourself, watching what comes out of your mouth or seeking the fourth step, wisdom. Prayer is a way God works in and through us to become an in-law pleasing to Him and others. Ask Him to grant you the wisdom to see opportunities which help you see how and when to open the gate.

The step to seeking wisdom is a big one. When we have done the other three steps and the gate's still shut, seek an older woman, pastor or counselor to help you see where you can improve. These four actions are valuable tools to keep from fencing others out prematurely as well as carefully searching for an obscure gate hidden in the fence erected to you. The issue you are experiencing just might be your in-law's fault, but you can see what lies in your power, and what does not, as you seek the wisdom to build or open.

## Lesson 7

# *Refrain From Answering an Accuser*

"**I** don't want to!" How many times did I say that to my own mother? Not one to negotiate, her firm reply was, "Do it anyway!" I must have been quite a sight standing ram rod straight with my stubborn stiff neck stating how ridiculous her demands on me were. I know I'm not the only one to cause their mother gray hair. A friend of mine's mom used to say to her, "Girl, you could wear down the Pope!"

More than once I added grays to Jean's precious head. She spent the net worth of a small nation coloring it during her tenure with me. One addition came as a result of a dinner conversation I had with the daughter of one of Jean's dearest friends. The daughter told me a funny story about her mother and I eagerly called Jean to jokingly share the tale. Jean was not amused. Her charm level dropped as she told me how painful this "story" had been for her friend.

People around town were laughing about the event and the mother was devastated. Jean was ashamed that I jumped on the gossip train at this woman's expense.

More than a little indignant, I reminded her it was this woman's daughter who had told *me* the story. A period of silence hung in the air and my words echoed in my ears. Realizing what I had done, I felt my pride balloon burst and asked myself, "Is this what I have become?"

Jean reminded me of her mother's words, "You can name names or tell tales, but you can't do both." In a matter of seconds I had stepped out of the person Jean knew and slipped on my old "so-n-so" cloak of years before. In those long shameful moments, I remembered who I was and apologized to my disappointed mother-in-law. In a way only a woman after God's heart can convey, she gently restored me by reminding me of the sorrow gossip causes and how the action never satisfies.

The friend who told the story on her mother, was also the child of an alcoholic, now saw me as someone who laughed at another's embarrassment. Our relationship would never become more than the superficial "no problems here" one we shared. Regretting my actions, I wondered when I would learn to lovingly place my arm around a shoulder while keeping one hand over my mouth. What a difference that action would have made, reflecting the Light that lived within me.

Maybe you are in an in-law relationship where the only commonality is talking about others. You know it's wrong and perhaps even started out inno-cently enough but now it has become your only bond. How do you un-ring the bell?

Your concern could challenge your patience level with those who accuse or fight to get in the last cutting word. How far would anyone expect you to go with this person who refuses to see any wrong in themselves when confrontation results in a barrage of insults?

This character flaw is not limited to in-laws. We may hide it better from those outside the family, but put us at the Thanksgiving Day table and it may natu-rally flow out unrestricted.

Pop culture asks, "WWJD? *What would Jesus do?*" in situations like my gossip encounter with Jean's friend's daughter. I can't guess what Jesus would do, I only know what Jesus *did* by reading Scripture. Falling short, as we all do, I decided to tweak WWJD to...What would *Jean* do? That was a little easier. After all, she set a high standard that, even today, I strive to achieve. She would encourage me to "pray without ceasing" and ask the Lord to show me the importance of keeping one hand over my mouth and evaluate my own feelings were I the one others laughingly told tales on. Well, this struck a chord. I had indeed been on the painful end of gossip more times than I would like to remember. I've spent many a tearful night grieving after discovering insen-sitive words spoken about me. Regardless if we are spoken harshly to by an accuser, or through gossip, the hurt contributes to how we respond to issues. The emotions from the pain can harden our responses causing us to act contrary to what we know is right.

How about you? Do you get with certain girl-friends and find yourself making comments about another? Maybe you heard a really funny story about a mutual acquaintance your friends would relate to and enjoy a common laugh at the predicament. There are a few thoughts we might want to evaluate about our motives for sharing a story. What was our purpose in repeating it? Was it to laugh at someone else's expense? Once the story is exposed do we feel some level of satisfaction? Maybe this is a good place to flip a few pages back to *Step One* is in order to do an attitude check and get an accurate view of yourself. Is there anyone you would *never* have told that story to? Contemplating this question brings to mind a few groups of people we would be ashamed to gossip to, yet something in us allows it to come to the surface with the closest of friends.

A few years back, during a party, a few friends and I were on the gossip train discussing someone we knew had divorced. It wasn't a secret and we were neither vicious nor judgmental but it opened a door for one of the women to say, "Oh, did you know Joe was divorced before he married his current wife?" All our mouths dropped open as this hidden truth was revealed and the room fell silent. One might think this not a harmful question, but no one *did* know this man had been married before and it wasn't our business to be told. The next day, this woman called the others and me to ask forgiveness for mentioning this man's position. When the room had gone quiet, her words brought about room for the Holy Spirit to convict her heart and she was remorseful. She saw the wrong and fought to rectify it quickly. Oh, that we would all be so sensitive to the wrongs we commit.

I often wonder why Jesus did not blast Pilate, the chief priests or King Herod when He stood falsely accused. He remained silent, but not defenseless. His silence spoke a crescendo of noise as His accusers were seen for what they were and Jesus was shown for what He was, the Savior of all.

Early in my days as women's ministries director of my church I listened, frozen and silent, in my office as an older woman presented a litany of my ministry shortcomings in monotonous detail. By the grace of God, I was able to thank her for coming and pray with her. But her words had cut deeper than I had ever been hurt. I felt berated and torn down. I was also MAD! Taking out a note pad, I wrote down every criticism I could remember her saying. I felt alone, attacked and cried out to God. "How could she be so unfair? If this is what serving women's ministries looked like, I'm bagging it!" The cost was just too great. I wanted to run to my husband for support but he was out of town. This hurt was too big to share over the phone so I decided not to tell him when he called. Bumping into one of our pastors a few hours later I gave him a brief synopsis of what transpired. He smiled and said, "Welcome to leadership!" I sank deeply into my office chair and realized he was right but desperately wanted him to say "let her have it." I wanted justification now!

Don't get me wrong, I'm no dummy. I knew there would be folks unhappy with my style of leadership, especially as changes occurred. I just had not expected it to hurt so much. I had worked to help ladies see the vision we were prayerfully casting and the need for instituting changes were all part of the package of progress. I signed up for this job with full knowledge I would face opposition. Through dependence on the Lord and wise counsel, I would grow through negative as well as the positive events that came my way. However, when it slapped me in the face, I wondered if I would survive.

I shut my door and prayed. I felt the peace of the Holy Spirit calm my heart which got me through the rest of the day. As night fell, so did my spirits. Those words spoken to me earlier came back over and over attacking my emotions and paralyzing my will to pray. I became restless as I worked up imaginary options for my response. Those options ranged from directing her to take a long walk off a short pier to giving her a dictionary with the definition of "exhorter" highlighted. I must admit I spent a little too much time on the pier scenario. I could see the wooden planks leading to the churning ocean below. I even saw faithful friends carrying her to the water's edge. In this warped fantasy of mine, she would turn from her evil ways and seek forgiveness just before she was thrown to a well-deserved watery grave. The crowds would cheer the heavens would part, and all creation would rejoice this one repented. We would all live happily ever after in our restored love for one another.

Still fretting in the night watches, I was aware my thinking was not healthy and certainly not from the Lord. The pain had me so encased; I felt like a trapped caterpillar in a decaying cocoon and continued questioning the validity of my calling. If this woman was unhappy with my leadership, maybe it wasn't my calling. I also wondered if she was gossiping about me to some of the other older ladies? At one time, I thought of her as a friend, but now she seemed like the enemy. "Where did this come from?" I asked as my pain consumed me. The things I knew to be true fell to the side as my bruised pride sought revenge. By letting the string and sting of her words repeat in my mind the anguish enveloped me tighter. Distraught, I continued my tirade until at some point during the night I gave up ownership to the Lord. What sweet communion washed over me once I laid my heart surrendered and broken at His feet. How much time I wasted I don't know, but sleep did finally come.

I awoke rested, refreshed and praising God for His mercies of the new day. My heart felt free of fear as He reminded me what this woman and I had in common, who we were in Christ's sight.

*"But you are a chosen race, a royal priesthood, a holy nation, a people for God's own possession, that you may proclaim the excellencies of Him who has called you out of darkness into His marvelous light."* I Peter 2:9

93

I can't speak for the Lord whether He thought either of us acted much like priests but I was grateful for the reminder we were His children and sisters in His family. The problem had not disappeared, but my attitude toward it changed. She and I were both His possessions and each had purpose in His kingdom.

Later that morning in my office, I asked the Lord if I could call a trusted friend to get her counsel on how to proceed. I believed His permission was granted and eagerly jumped from my knees to contact her. Throwing open my office door, I shrieked with delight to see this very friend standing there! Tears welled up in my eyes as a not so delighted shriek came from her when I pulled her into a startled hug. She said she just *happened* to be at the church that morning and thought she would stop by to say hi. She sat amazed as I told her how the Lord had placed her in that exact spot to show me His sovereign faithfulness and love that morning.

I explained what happened the day before and asked her to pray with me. When we finished, my friend encouraged me to look over the accusations to see if there was any truth to the woman's words. I felt my anxiety rise again. I did not say it, but my heart's response screamed, "I don't want to!" Images of the woman walking the plank returned, but I told my friend I would do as she suggested. Rats! Now what?

I knew she was right, but I called Jean instead. Surely she would give me comfort and tell me to call out the friends for the parade to the pier. Hardly. Jean asked if I had asked the Lord if there was any truth to the accusations. What? How did she know my friend had asked me to pray the same thing? I never wanted to see that list again! Resigned, I chose to believe these two admonitions came from the Lord. I did not want to but knew the Lord instructed me to do it anyway.

Slowly, I picked up the pad and carefully looked at each entry. My prayer was to hold a humbling magnifying mirror up to get an accurate view of myself. Surprise! There *were* areas of weakness and, OUCH, pride. Yes, this woman's presentation could have used some work. And, in my wounded state, it seemed it lacked the encouragement and love I would have preferred, but by the healing hand of God this painful experience enlarged my faith and dependence on Him. I gained a greater love for the women of our ministry and a special love for this messenger of His. I believe God sent her because I might not have listened to a more gentle confrontation.

Even with this assurance from God this was for my good, I still wanted a little vindication so I looked up the definition of "exhort" in the Encarta Dictionary. Exhort was defined as a verb:

1. **Urge to do something** – to urge somebody strongly and earnestly to do something
2. **Give earnest advice** – to give somebody urgent or earnest advice

All self righteous thoughts were dashed as I understood she had done exactly what God had called her to do. I also realized her confrontation was in love even though I could not see it at the time. She had indeed "exhorted" me. She *had* urged me strongly and earnestly to be careful in my service to God's women.

What happened to the woman? I'm happy to say my fantasy never materialized. She is one of our church's most faithful servants with a direct approach for encouraging few others can compare. I saw this wasn't about me but about her great love for God in her desire to protect our women. I learned she had just cause to be cautious because of some damaging actions inflicted on women years before by another leader. She was now "on guard" to prevent it from happening again. Although I didn't enjoy the trial, the Lord used it for the good of His ministry. It was His ministry after all, not mine.

Application starts here, ladies. All of us have situations where we *think* we are in the right. This woman and I both thought we were 100% right. Yet, with sweet wisdom from two women outside the circumstance, and by refraining from answering an accuser, the Holy Spirit worked in me. How He works in others is up to Him.

> *"...Jesus our Lord, equip you in every good thing to do His will, working in us that which is pleasing in His sight, through Jesus Christ, to whom be the glory forever and ever. Amen"*
> Hebrews 13:20b-21

This same Jesus is available to equip each of us in our interaction with in-laws to do good things according to His will, things that are pleasing in His sight. On the other hand, if we choose not to accept the equipping we are constrained to present and receive communication with chips on our shoulders. Those chips obstruct us from asking if there are any kernels of truth in the words spoken to us. Perhaps like the woman in my office an instance from another time may have caused distrust? Maybe confrontation is indeed needed but is rejected due to a poor presentation. That chip can be a terrible barrier to the Holy Spirit's working in our lives. Maybe like me, the Lord will use a stronger approach because we would never hear it otherwise.

So often, life experiences can jade our reactions to others leaving our responses "less than cordial." We have to fill ourselves with God's word.

*"Thy word I have treasured in my heart, that I may not sin against Thee."* Psalm 119:11

Shortly before Jean died, she eagerly told me she had a new book for me by Jan Karon, called **The Continual Feast.** This book of inspirational quotes, verses, and poems had motivated her to pray and praise and she wanted to be sure I knew I should read it. When her death came I gently placed it with the other items she had left in a pile reserved for me. It was months before I picked the book up to find why she was so emphatic it was for me. Granted, I had heard it was a great book from many, but why Jean made a point of telling me I did not know until I opened the book and began to read. She knew I was struggling with a "chip" on my shoulder so she left me a special message which helped that chip be removed forever.

In those last few weeks, Jean knew she was dying. There was so much she wanted to say to so many: her husband, sons, grandsons; grandsons' wives; brother; sister-in-law; and me, to name a few. Too much to say and too little time, she chose a more subtle way to get her message across. She had marked in pencil a little "x" on pages that held a special meaning for her. As I read the words of Christ's influence on the lives of His people and how the enduring words of Scripture were gently marked with an "x", a lump the size of a ham hock rose in my throat. God had used these verbal treasures to carry her through her final days and now they spoke her good-bye words of wisdom to carry me, too. Jean marked the following which portrays…WWJD, not only what Jesus would do, but also what Jean would do.

## THE PARADOXICAL COMMANDMENTS
### By Kent M. Keith

1. *People are illogical, and self-centered. Love them anyway.*
2. *If you do good, people will accuse you of selfish, ulterior motives. Be good anyway.*
3. *If you are successful, you will win false friends and true enemies. Succeed anyway.*
4. *The good you do today will be forgotten tomorrow. Do good anyway.*
5. *Honesty and frankness make you vulnerable. Be honest and frank anyway.*
6. *The biggest men and women with the biggest ideas can be shot down by the smallest men and women with the smallest minds. Think big anyway.*
7. *People favor underdogs but follow only top dogs. Fight for a few underdogs anyway.*
8. *What you spend years building may be destroyed overnight. Build anyway.*
9. *People really need help but may attack you if you do help them. Help people anyway.*
10. *Give the world the best you have and you'll get kicked in the teeth. Give the world the best you have anyway.*

You see, in the final analysis, it is between you and God. It was never between you and them anyway.

## Lesson 8

# *Be Aware of the Mark You Leave*

When I was a kid, I didn't like to get dirty. If I scraped my knee I was devastated. I preferred my clothes clean and my legs Band-Aid free. To this day I can remember every incident for every scar. Like the one inch scar on my right foot from a rusted, dirty wire that caught me while running through a friend's yard. Then I remember an unattractive, but thankfully small, scar on the left side of my nose. It happened during a game of tag when I was 11. I was attempting a strategic move to dodge the tag when my pursuer matched my move with a mighty slap of her hand. In that split-second action, her fingernail got me with a two inch slicing swipe to my nose. Even though she was only 10, she was a big girl with what I thought were giant's hands. Blood gushed as she smiled and said, "That's gonna leave a mark!" I wanted to punch her, but fear of another lash of those "man hands" sealed my lips tight.

If I had power to choose whether to receive scars or not...I would choose not. My physical scars aren't the only marks inflicted on me. My early childhood years were full of laughter, but one day the laughter stopped. It happened in the tumultuous 60s: full of drugs, sit-ins and a changing world. My father's company couldn't keep up and was forced to close their doors. He had planned to be with them till retirement. Instead, this WWII veteran struggled with how to provide for his family in the midst of unfamiliar territory. Bourbon became his closest friend; a friend that took his fears and masked them as everyone else's problem. Each evening I pleaded with him not to drink that night but he would avert his eyes and take another sip. In time, my mother joined in his alcoholic friendship. My older brother, sister and I began to comprehend things in our family would never be the same. The life we knew had vaporized before us, forever.

Times were not only tough on our family but the entire country. The South was slowly transforming for African-Americans from the land of oppression to the hope of equality. Civil Rights marches and tensions in Atlanta grew hotter than an August night while my father's prejudice grew equally heated and explosive. His actions divulged a man I had never known. He had always been so kind. Now he drank, cursed and spoke harshly to our housekeeper. When I asked what made him so angry, he blamed it on the "Blacks and Jews" of our city. As I grew older, I could see how much he based his limited self-respect solely in a culture filled with false superiority. Alteration in a society he thought he knew left him with an unwillingness to accept or adapt himself to the changing times. This different dad shook my security. I was scared. The man I counted on to protect and guide me had now deserted me, emotionally.

Too young to understand how alcoholism can change a person's disposition, and severely damage a family, I somehow hoped he would miraculously become the daddy he used to be. The one I needed. My mother refused to address his drinking by bluntly instructing me to keep what happened in our home, in our home. No one may know. I was alone in my trepidation. Anxiety became part of my temperament since I was fearful of this new father. His evening rants led me to a fear of the world as well. A disturbing scar had been slashed in to my heart and left an unseen mark.

During those same years, another young girl's father was making a mark on her life. Our paths crossed my freshman year of high school. Yogi and I were on the pep squad together at Grady High School, in Atlanta. The racial tension was painfully high in our school and fights became a common occurrence. During an exceptionally vicious clash in our lunchroom, I ran to the school office frightened and told the principal I could not spend another day there. He called my mother as I cleaned out my locker.

Yogi stopped by my locker, as I cleared out my things, to ask what I was doing. I told her, "*I am scared at home, now scared at school and I'm leaving."* She looked me in the eye and said, *"Mimi, if you run from your fears, they will own you."* As her words were still hanging in the air, she quietly turned and walked away.

Yogi knew something about fear. She had faced it many times in her young life. A few years before she spoke those words to me, she had received the news her father had been shot and killed as he stood on a hotel balcony in Memphis. Yogi was Yolanda King and her father was Dr. Martin Luther King, Jr. She knew fear.

Two girls, two fathers, two marks: one white, one African-American. My father left a mark of bigotry on all who knew him, Dr. King changed the world. Yogi's father left a mark of legacy on his daughter and she in turn left a mark on me that prompted the courage to face my fears so many years ago and to this day.

My mother-in-law left a mark on me, too. Those 28 years patterning a life of loving lessons are tattooed onto my heart, my mind and my soul. When Jean was diagnosed with cancer the second time, I desperately wanted her to mark me up with every drop of loving ink she had left. I thought of all the phone calls I should have made over the years and now just wanted to go to her. The day she called to say she would be starting aggressive treatment I assumed I would fly to Tennessee to help care for her. Jean said no. They would let me know if they needed me. I was crushed. That's not the mark I wanted.

Absorbed in my sense of rejection, I did what I always do when my feelings are hurt...I pulled weeds!

It took about an hour of pity-party weed clearing before I sat down in the dirt and sobbed. *Lord, why can't I go? Why doesn't she want me there? I want to be with her. I want to sit by her during chemo. I want to hold her hand. I want MORE!*

The answer from Him came clearly. I had already been given the best Jean had to give me. This was her choice to make and she had chosen it as a time to minister to, and be encouraged by, others. It was their turn, not mine. Even as my heart cried no, I knew the Lord had called Jean's legacy to continue. She had others to leave marks on. This time was not for or about me.

Following her death, I heard stories from nurses, doctors and other patients where her ink had penetrated into their lives. One mark was on her primary doctor who wrote me saying, "I thought very highly of Mrs. Moseley. I will always remember her with a smile on her face and a very upbeat and cheerful attitude. It was a pleasure to spend time with her and I will remember her fondly." I thought of what a tough job this doctor had and how difficult it must be to see most of his patients die. Yet this one gave him what he needed to come back to work the next day and try again.

A short time ago, I had the honor of speaking at the memorial service of another woman that marked my life with lessons of love. I met Theresa Vogt when I was in fourth grade. I had just begun riding lessons and she was the instructor, and owner, of the riding academy I attended. This woman and her husband had fled war torn Germany in 1952, and opened stables in

Atlanta two years later. Her story uniquely attracted me. Not only was she an immigrant, Theresa was a devoted wife, mother and a mentor to the hundreds of young girls and boys that came through her barn over the years. She worked hard to be a woman of character.

Theresa's teaching spread beyond the riding ring to lessons on loving. In my early teen years, I began aligning myself with girls outside the academy. The girls were more interested in the temporal and tacky, than in the quality stature Theresa strived to instill in her students. This new demeanor showed itself in the way I treated my friend, her daughter, Anneliese. I began to ignore Anneliese in lieu of impressing my new friends and Theresa was *not* amused. I had changed. The loving voice I often heard and craved from Theresa disappeared, replaced with one of fire. I stood humiliated as this little German woman with hands on hips challenged me. I had crossed a line and she loved me enough to tell me how I had disappointed her. Her voice was full of disgust and impatience as she walked away mumbling strong words in German. I did not need to understand the language her tone spoke clearly.

Theresa's admonition broke my heart. This woman, my heroine, would not tolerate my actions. After a long pouting session, I returned with a repentant heart. She had built a hedge between us in an effort to set a boundary, but in her wisdom, left a gate. She made a choice to forgive me and showed grace unlike anything I had ever known. In time, I learned to show this grace to others. I could see the legacy the Lord had woven through her life. The mark she left on me was a beauty mark. Which mark will I leave on my daughters-in-law and other women who cross my path?

What legacy are you leaving? A scar or a beauty mark? How will *you* be remembered? What are *you* teaching younger women? Are you leaving marks that show love and forgiveness or scars of resentment and bitterness? We leave marks on each other regardless if inflicted purposely or not. But the mark does not have to be a reminder of pain. Jesus can take those scars and use them for His glory. You have a choice: Do you pull up your sleeve, point to the scar and get all worked up again about the pain and anguish or do you pull up that sleeve, state what the scar was and then victoriously say, *"Let me tell you what Jesus did with that pain."* Yeah, the scar will still be there, but now it has purpose to show what Jesus did. Use that lesson to encourage in-laws and other women to tell how you lived through your pain and what you learned through the healing.

When Jesus appeared to the disciples after His resurrection, His scars remained. A special purpose allowed those marks to be visible. A special purpose allowed those marks to be visible. That purpose was to show them and the world what He had done for us. It left a mark.

*"And He Himself bore our sins in His body on the cross, that we might die to sin and live to righteousness; for by His wounds you were healed."* I Peter 2:24

## Lesson 9

# *Choose to Love*

In 2004, the movie *"Lost in Translation"* was credited as, "the best movie of the year." I never saw it, but I understand it was the story of a depressed has-been actor traveling to Japan for work. He discovers how lost he is with the language, thus equally realizing how lost he is with his life, too.

I imagine some of you reading this book may be left with the same lost feeling in regards to your in-law relationship. You've tried every suggestion I have listed, and many others, only to discover what you already knew, that in-law of yours is just impossible. You wonder how your husband could have come from this woman or you struggle to believe how that precious baby boy of yours could have found someone as unfit as your daughter-in-law.

During my research, I interviewed many women floating in just such a lifeboat to nowhere feeling hopeless with their in-law relationships. Many strived to find the root cause only to be rewarded with mistrust or painful attacks and now ask, "How can I possibly "choose to love" *her*?

Jean and I knew we would not be able to write this book without addressing this aspect of hopelessness. Although I've heard over 100 stories, I will only touch on three. Maybe you can step into their stories and imagine what it might be like to walk in their shoes. How did they earn these impossible burdens? Some of you are carrying just such difficult afflictions right now and I challenge you to consider if something in these stories might help you make the choice to love your in-law.

The stories you will read are true, but just like in the old detective TV shows, "the names have been changed to protect the innocent." Be cautious as you read. King David took up the offensive at the hearing of the prophet Nathan's story in II Samuel 12, demanding that man should surely die, only to be told he was the man at fault. Consider how you may relate to these characters.

### Evie & Aimee

Evie was the middle child of her family and suffered from the jealous feeling of favoritism her father showed her older sister. Evie made good grades, went to college and married a smart man who loved her. However, she never felt she measured up in her father's eyes. Evie's sister and her family continued to be shining lights as Evie persisted in her life-long self-fulfilling prophecy of failure. Her husband divorced her after 20 years of marriage leaving her and two children alone.

A few years after the divorce, Evie's son brought home the girl he wanted to marry, Aimee. Evie turned cold and said Aimee was not right for him. Aimee's education consisted of only a short time at a community college before she decided to leave school without a degree and work instead. Both of Evie's sister's children had married college graduates and she desperately wanted her children's spouses to "show well," too. It didn't help that Evie's father thought Aimee was a delight, welcoming her warmly into the family. Evie lashed out wanting someone to blame. Aimee unknowingly was branded with an invisible target on her back.

Well placed, catty remarks let Aimee know who ruled the family. As the "daughter-in-law," Aimee must comprehend she had no voice in family matters. Her son had never understood his mother and offered no help to his new bride. Little by little, Aimee began to employ a defensive front that added fuel to Evie's fire until Aimee finally gave up on all attempts to communicate with her.

As a follower of Christ, this conflict made Aimee feel like a failure and hopeless that she could not bridge the gap to her mother-in-law. Lost in this relationship, Aimee began to pray. "Please, Lord, move Evie to another country or at least another town!" Either option was fine with Aimee. She knew her prayers were a bit twisted and slowly began to surrender this relationship to the Lord. She asked Him to show her what made Evie so difficult and pleaded with Jesus to show her something in her mother-in-law she could love. Now she was on the right track. Aimee began to notice the tension battled between Evie and her father. She observed how Evie actions belied a second class citizen spot in the family. Family members became weary of Evie's complaints and attitudes, yet she continued to be abrasive.

It took years, but little by little God answered Aimee's prayers in breaking up her own fallow ground until compassion became her soil and a bud of love sprouted for this woman. Aimee saw loving Evie as an offering and a sacrifice pleasing to God.

> *"And walk in love, just as Christ also loved you, and gave Himself up for us, an offering and a sacrifice to God as a fragrant aroma."*
> Ephesians 5:2

Evie's self-destructive behavior didn't change but Aimee's heart did. She chose to love her anyway, unsure there would ever be a reward for her efforts.

As Evie lay dying in a care facility, Aimee alone visited sitting through the sour words about the family day after day, yet striving to show and tell Evie of Christ's love. Finally came the day Aimee never thought she would see. Evie reached out her hand to her and apologized for her harshness to her all those years. She told Aimee she was the only person in her family that ever showed her love and acceptance. Aimee gently smiled and stroked Evie's hand as tears of joy filled her eyes. Evie did notice! She knew her striving had not been in vain as she said, *"Oh, Evie, you are most forgiven."* The next day Evie died. Aimee never knew if Evie accepted Christ, but she did know she made a difference by sacrificing herself for another and the guilt-free assurance of no regrets.

What a wasted life Evie experienced. In constant need of affirmation she undermined her own actions thus alienating those she desired to love her. What blessing she missed.

*"By wisdom a house is built, and by under-standing it is established; and by knowledge the rooms are filled with all precious and pleasant riches."* Proverbs 24:3-4

These riches Jean lavished on me filled a store-house of resources set aside for me as I began to understand wisdom, sacrifice and the choice to love.

### Shar and Adrian

Shar was thrilled when her son brought Adrian home to meet the family. She was beautiful, articulate and obviously crazy about Shar's son. Within months of the wedding, Adrian's love-craziness toward her husband turned to domination and exclusion of his family. If Shar called, Adrian would say her husband wasn't available and take a message. During family gatherings, if Shar and her son were alone for any length of time, Adrian would show up and pull him away claiming an important matter in need of his attention. Adrian rarely invited Shar and her husband to her home except for an event where

Adrian's family would also be present. Once grandchildren were born, invitations came even less often giving preferential treatment to her parents.

As time wore on, bitterness grew in Shar's heart and animosity bloomed. She complained to her son and he defended his wife. Helpless, hurt and angry, Shar buried her pain and lived this life of rejection. *"A son is a son until he takes a wife. A daughter is a daughter, the rest of her life."* Hearing this old adage from a friend, added salt to her wounds. What happened to her sweet son? Is her relationship with him gone forever?

Shar spent her days going through the motions until the day her ears perked up listening to a Christian radio talk show. The person hosting the show was talking about healing from various pains. He said we make a choice to heal and quoted John 5:6, when Jesus asked the man, *"Do you want to get well?"* It seemed like a silly question, but a light bulb came on in her. Shar saw she had been feeding off her pain with a diet of misery that left her weak and hopeless. Almost out loud she said, "Yes, I want to be well!" and after listening further with careful consideration attended a conference on the subject.

Shar came home a changed woman. She had been miserable for years and blamed it all on her daughter-in-law. Not only had she alienated her son, she had shared her poison with her husband infecting him, too. Like the man in the John 5 verse who had been sick for so long, Shar felt she heard Jesus ask her if she wanted to be well. This sickness had progressed too far for her to heal herself. She received the needed

help from godly professionals and began to implement what she had learned by forgiving Adrian for
the years of rejection. She also pledged to pray for
healthy interaction with her daughter-in-law.

Shar remembered many encounters followed by
silent tears as she chose to obey the Lord. The words
of the Psalmist especially touched her in this effort.

> *"Those who sow in tears shall reap with joyful*
> *shouting. He who goes to and fro weeping,*
> *carrying his bag of seed, shall indeed come*
> *again with a shout of joy, bringing his sheaves*
> *with him."* Psalm 126:5-6

She did grieve over the loss of her dream, a loving
relationship with her daughter-in-law, but day by day
she stood firm, content in knowing God was going to
have glory in this situation. She chose to be a good
example to her son and daughter-in-law regardless
of anything in return. When Adrian's grandmother
died, Shar took a meal, wrote a kind card and made
herself available as needed. That day Adrian saw her
mother-in-law for the first time as a friend. Little by
little Adrian began to respond to Shar's actions, but
the *joyful shouting* was elusive. It did finally come
a few years later when Adrian attended a women's
retreat with her church. During the Saturday evening
portion of the message, the speaker shared a testimony of unforgiveness in her own life and how it had
damaged those around her accomplishing nothing but
a hindrance between her and the Lord. The speaker
encouraged the women to take a look at their life

and pondor, *was unforgiveness holding them back?*
When the speaker prayed in closing, Adrian knew
not only was Shar the person she needed to forgive,
but more so, was the one in whom she needed to ask
forgiveness.

Arriving home, Adrian told her husband and
they prayed for God's perfect opportunity to talk to
Shar. The memories and animosity between them
had created a daunting chasm. Adrian took a step
toward that divide and contacted Shar for a meeting.
Awkwardly, she tripped over rushed sentences mostly
in an effort to defend why she had behaved the way
she had all these years putting indirect blame on Shar.
Over the course of tears and some accusations Shar
remained silent, listening.

Adrian said she had felt extreme jealousy because
her husband had often compared her to Shar. He had
been Shar's darling boy and Adrian felt the compe-
tition. She went on to say she felt like an outsider
when Shar would constantly bring up stories from
his childhood that made everyone knowingly laugh
except her. Surprisingly, Adrian saw her mother-in-
law's eyes fill with tenderness and tears of her own.
Shar confessed a level of truth in Adrian's words.
The more Shar's daughter-in-law had rejected her,
the more she tried to hold onto to something in her
son's life by reminiscing at family gatherings about
him before knowing Adrian. *That* was the reason she
and her husband's invitations for visits were limited?
Could it be this "under the radar" battle was indeed
intentional on both their parts?

Both examined themselves and saw areas where each had caused hurt. They realized they traveled on the same road, loved the same people and that was enough to start loving each other.

I'm happy to tell you, today, these two women are making it. It's not perfect, but progress has been made. They decided they would rather walk on a few eggshells with each other than not be on the same road at all. This took work. It took confession and it took getting an accurate view of their motives and themselves.

Have you been prodded by the Holy Spirit to examine yourself? Surely there is plenty of blame to go around, and your in-law certainly has her share, but what are *you* responsible for? That's all the Lord is asking of you. Let him take care of the other person. Seek forgiveness for your part regardless of whether they respond or not. Your bondage will be freed and that's where you need to begin. Once exposed to the light it won't have the power it had when hidden in the darkness.

## Cindy & Tammy

Cindy was a pillar of the church. Her love for her family and commitment to God was evident to all. If one imagines a "perfect family" she seemed to have it. Cindy's son made good choices. He graduated from college in less than four years, landed a successful position in his field of study and had the world by the tail. His job took him to Southern California where he poured himself into his work.

117

Two years later, Tammy walked into his life. She rocked his world and changed everything. Her carefree spirit and quick wit charmed him with a love he had never known. They fell head over heels in love and moved in together after dating only a few months. He knew his parents would not approve so when he called home, which was less and less, he made excuses why his parents should not visit, but he came home instead.

Cindy had no reason to worry simply assuming her son was working hard in his career. Worry came when she received his phone call announcing his marriage to Tammy. Not only was he married, she hadn't even met this girl that was now her daughter-in-law. He and Tammy would be home that weekend so the family could meet their newest member.

Blindsided by the news, Cindy dropped to her chair and cried. How could he have done this? Her first born responsible well-grounded son! This girl must have seduced him. A flood of wedding scenes she would never experience evaporated before her mind's eye replaced with visions of telling friends what had happened. Anger at her son, suspicion of this new "daughter-in-law" and a sense of betrayal from God enveloped her. "God, you could have kept this from happening!" she wept accusingly. Hadn't she been a faithful servant of the Lord? What kind of reward was this?

When Cindy's husband walked in the door a few minutes later the floodgates broke loose until she sunk to the floor exhausted in his arms. They had two days to prepare themselves for what her son had said would be a celebration.

The two days ended too quickly. Dread clouded the morning as they waited for the "newly-weds" to arrive. Cindy, her husband and their other two children sat silently. She felt like a caged lion. She could not even pray. Everything within her wanted to slam the door on this young woman and bring her son back to his senses.

The sound of a car door closing brought Cindy back to the present. She and her husband exchanged a foreboding look as they opened the door to her precious baby boy who boldly walked in with his wife. Introductions were uneasy as each family member tentatively shook Tammy's hand. She smiled and tried to act happy to meet them, but was well aware of the judgmental looks in their eyes.

Excusing the younger siblings, Cindy invited her son and Tammy to join her and her husband in the living room. After a few minutes of strained small-talk questions of Tammy's family, Cindy could stand it no longer and tearfully said, "How could you hurt your parents and us so badly?" The room turned cold as the two women stared each other down. Tammy countered with well rehearsed words from the Bible instructing a man to leave his father and mother and cleave to his wife, her tone firm and direct. Any form of civility begun was shattered as attacking battle lines formed on each woman's face. Cindy's husband tried to calm the emotions, but the war had begun and neither side would back down. Raging with anger son and Tammy left the door open as they fled to their car returning to Southern California. Cindy could not remember ever being so angry or hurt so bad. She was appalled that *they* were mad. Cindy and her husband were the offended ones.

Two weeks passed after their first encounter. Father and son spent time on the phone determining a trip down south was needed. With strong urging from her husband, Cindy reluctantly agreed. Now, they would meet on Tammy's turf. Anger welled up within her as they reached for the doorbell. Tight lipped they crossed the threshold of the condominium Tammy and her son shared into an atmosphere heavy with dread on both sides. In the last two weeks, Cindy's friends had fostered her anger just as Tammy's friends had taken up her offense. Two women prepared for their second battle.

Shortly after they seated themselves Cindy's husband asked, *"First, before we say another word, I would like to pray."* He reached over and put his hand on Cindy's arm and sadly watched as she squirmed away from his touch. She wanted to get the guns out and start firing. After all, she was the victim here. But as he prayed, the tension of a war room melted and soothing words calmed hot emotions.

For the most part, as Tammy and her son began expressing their reasons for eloping, Cindy and her husband sat quietly and listened. Then the other shoe dropped. A startling new element had been added. Not only did they have a new daughter-in-law, but they would soon become grandparents. This new turn just about did Cindy in. Searching her son's face for confirmation, she finally comprehended as reality broke through. Her energy zapped, and the peace of her husband's prayer broken, she picked up her purse, walked out their door and waited alone in the car.

The remaining three exchanged awkward glances. Again stung by Cindy's rejection, Tammy pushed away her husband's hand of comfort but listened to his father ask them to consider what Cindy was feeling. This big and totally unexpected news had plummeted her into shock, *"give her some time to process it all",* he pleaded. Then, turning to his son, he reminded him of his mother's character and love. That had not changed, just been temporarily derailed. Hugging both, he walked to the car for the very long trip home.

Tammy's own mother Pam had not been receptive either by their quick marriage, regardless of the reasons. She too had been cheated out of her child's wedding and had taken Cindy's side. She wrote a letter to Cindy sharing her own pain and disappointment. Pam and Cindy had little in common except their children who had married, and each was about to become a first time grandmother, so they decided to meet.

Their meeting started well, but turned quickly. Calling it "ill at ease" would have been an understatement. The look on Pam's face spoke clear and painfully to Cindy. Instead of meeting an ally, she saw her own negative responses to Pam's daughter mirrored back to her as Pam rejected this new "son-in-law" and cast the blame of this mess on him. Her words about Cindy's son were exactly how she felt about Tammy. She had chosen to look at Tammy as an intruder to her life and refused to view her any other way.

Cindy was no different than Pam. The love and acceptance she received from the Lord was sorely missing in her relationship with this new daughter-in-law. Could she possibly share some of the responsibility for the strain due to withholding love from Tammy? She cried out to the Lord and asked how she could undo her part in this conflict. She knew the Lord would want this yet a self-righteousness attitude reared its head once more as her flesh screamed for her own rights. Cindy opened God's Word and asked for help. The love of God was woven into everything she read. The call to love seemed to be repeated everywhere she looked. There was no ignoring His message to her.

> *"Wherefore, accept one another, just as Christ also accepted us to the glory of God."*
> Romans 15:7

Returning home, she wrestled with the desire to cling to her anger but all the while seeing the damage already done. Finally, in the quiet of her bedroom, she surrendered her rights to the Lord and picked up the phone. A sense of relief washed over her when Tammy's voicemail picked up. Cindy almost hung up, but left a message instead. She told Tammy she desperately wanted to talk and closed her message with, "I hope we can start over."

Two days went by before Cindy made another attempt to call. This time Tammy answered and listened with distrustful and distant ears to Cindy's words. Cindy began by admitting she knowingly rejected Tammy and even at first blamed her for seducing her son away from the life he was meant to live. Cindy then added she was so sorry for these feelings and for her actions that contributed to a bad beginning as a new mother-in-law. She asked for forgiveness and asked Tammy if she could have a second chance. She also wanted to share in the excitement of the first grandchild.

Tammy could hardly speak for the emotion in her throat, but finally stated the words Cindy had longed to hear. Tammy acknowledged Cindy had the dream most mothers do of a wedding full of family and friends and asked her forgiveness for taking that dream from her. Both women sobbed on each end of the phone until nervous laughter broke through. Cindy invited Tammy to come back to visit and be welcomed properly into the family. Today Cindy and Tammy are good friends. No one would have blamed either woman for holding a grudge against the other. Instead, a deep love has grown from their scarred battlefield.

These three stories are unique and yet have one thing in common. One of the in-laws in each situation made a decision to take a challenge from God and trust Him for the result. Can relationships, like these, work for people that are not followers of Christ? Of course, but each of these women would say what a blessing they could have missed had the Creator of the world not been intimately involved in their lives and helped them choose love.

## Lesson 10

# *We All Need "Peach"*

During Jean's teaching years with junior high students she often found the need to speak one on one with a parent regarding their child's progress. Desmond was a delightful boy, but struggled with a speech impediment requiring Jean to ask him to repeat himself. She knew he needed some special classes and asked Desmond to tell his mother she would like to meet with her. The message never seemed to make it home. Finally, an appointment was set and Desmond's mother came to a meeting.

Upon entering the room, she introduced herself. To Jean's shock, she could not understand much of what the mother said. She asked her to repeat herself but still struggled to figure out what she had said. The mother also had a speech impediment. Desmond's mother was as sweet as he was and Jean found herself drawn to this woman as she exerted all her concentration to follow the mother as she spoke.

Jean addressed the educational challenges Desmond experienced and asked his mother what she thought would be best. Her answer caught Jean off-guard, *"I think he needs peach!"* Jean smiled and said that yes a "speech" class would be a good option and made the arrangements.

Driving home she couldn't help thinking of the woman's words and smiled. Jean thought how true the statement was and how *"We all need peach!"* The words we say can be misinterpreted by those that don't understand us. It takes a level of effort to deduce what our in-law is trying to say. Her words may come out in a way that gives an entirely different meaning than what they intended. Your words may be perceived incorrectly, too. We all need to practice our "peach".

It takes a humble heart to admit we might be the one who needs to speak differently. During my years in women's ministries speaking to variety of women's groups required I watch the words I use. I remember the time I delivered a message to the leadership team of a women's conference the day before the main portion of the conference began. During my message, I mentioned there may be attendees the next day who are quite content to be where they are in their spiritual walks. Unfortunately, I used the old cliché they could be *"fat, dumb and happy"* in their walks. When my talk ended a woman came up and said she thought my words could be hurtful to women by calling them fat or dumb. The other women standing with me were shocked to discover she had never heard that cliché before. Of course I would never call God's women fat or dumb, it was just a saying. But if she had not come and asked me, she would have questioned my love for women.

How often do we just rush ahead to make assumptions and judgments by choosing not to ask for clarification? It's your call. From the beginning of this book, I have said this is not a "how to" book, but a "you have a choice" book. Your in-law may not be what you had hoped for but is what you have, and the question is, *"What are you going to do about it?*

My friend, Kent Nichols' mother-in-law, Melva Nichols suggests ten applications of loving lessons to try. Each is an action or choice we can incorporate into our lives right now.

1. **Set an example and stick to it.** Determine that you will live a good example to your in-law on a long term basis.
2. **Talk often and show interest in their lives.** Regardless of whether she reciprocates, call just to say hi and see what is new in her life.
3. **Ask how you can help.** If you know she has a project coming up, ask if you can do anything to help lighten the load.
4. **Forgive quickly**. This is difficult and you may do this repeatedly. It is good to remember how often the Lord forgives you.
5. **Look for God's purpose in every trial.** He has a reason for the trial, so start looking! You may not see it at the time, that is when you chose to believe He is working without seeing.

6. **Take a little something to her on every visit.** It doesn't have to be big or expensive. How about bringing her a genuine smile?
7. **Mail a note even if you live in the same town.** This is easy and cheap.
8. **Let God be your defense.** Vengeance is His alone. You will only get yourself in trouble trying to fix or retaliate.
9. **Remember hurt lies in each of us.** She has a reason to act the way she does. Hurt people, *hurt*.
10. **You are accountable**. God is the one you will give an answer to for your actions. Choose to love.

*"A gentle answer turns away wrath, but a harsh word stirs up anger."* Proverbs 15:1

*"Pride goes before destruction, and a haughty spirit before stumbling."* Proverbs 16:18

God's word will serve you well. He is faithful to be with you, know you and hear you when you call. Remember His word will light the path you walk. But we must watch our steps...Just when we feel the most self-righteous and put upon, we can say something stupid proving we all need "peach".

Jean felt strongly that seeing ourselves for the flawed creatures we are can help us in these loving lessons for mothers and daughters-in-law. When she and I shared a platform for an in-law relationship seminar many questions came in that we did not have time to answer. As we looked through those heart-felt questions, Jean realized we could answer them in this book. So here, in her own words, Jean shares some more of her in-law communication wisdom:

I believe the best advice you can give is in the word of God. My answers below are from an imperfect woman. Tarnished and yet called by God in Titus two to encourage younger women. I'm older than most women, so this is for you all!

## Question: How can I deal with a mother-in-law who is totally self-centered and suspicious of my efforts to live in harmony with her?

Our attitudes toward others are often formed early in life. Your mother-in-law is probably suspicious of many people and afraid of being hurt. Chances are you are not being singled out, just more assessable. Dig down a little and see if perhaps she was neglected emotionally as a child or even spoiled. She may be manipulative and sees herself reflected in others, suspecting their motives. Dishonest, selfish people expect these traits in everyone else. Try to bear with her and don't lose your sense of humor. You may need it to survive. You don't have to be her fall guy. Limit your time together and don't forget to PRAY!

## Question: How do you deal with a mother-in-law who is unstable to the point of being dangerous with the grandchildren?

If you feel the grandchildren are due for a visit, put a safety measure in place. First determine if there is a time she seems "better". Are mornings better than

Saturday nights? If she is an alcoholic, mornings are usually their good times when they are on their best behavior. Some older people run out of steam in the afternoons and become grumpy. Look for ways to make her time with the children successful, but be smart. It is your responsibility to be sure the children are safe. If you are truly as concerned as you seem, plan visits that include you, your husband or another trusted adult. If you plan enough of these visits and outings you may wear her out to the point she's too beat to want the kids alone.

Push may come to shove with an insistent grandma. In that case, your husband should be the boundary setter. Discuss the safety issue in depth with him. Then be sure he understands he should speak to his mother from his position and **not** speaking for you. Encourage him to be confident to stand his ground. Then PRAY!

**Question: The Bible gives us an example of an in-law relationship between Naomi and Ruth. Why do daughters-in-law fail to respect their mothers-in-law and not follow what the Bible says?**

I can only answer as an older woman and a mother-in-law and what I know of this story. Ruth was a loving woman, obedient to God. She is also named as an ancestor of Jesus. Ruth lived in a Middle Eastern culture that taught respect for elders. Unfortunately, America has slipped far since the last century with attitudes of inconvenience in the care and respect of elderly family members. There is a sense of disdain when younger ones mock and devalue grandparents and older people. God's children must set the example as respectful models to their children and their friends as well as the grandparents. If you speak of your parent as a pain, your child will pick up on that and do the same. Respect of elders is sadly lacking in today's generation and many Christian families are guilty of failing to raise polite respectful kids.

As a mother-in-law, I want to pause and speak to fellow mothers-in-law. Some of you are doing a great job of encouraging the younger women to:

> *"...love their husbands, to love their children, to be sensible, pure, workers at home, kind, being subject to their own husbands, that the word of God may not be dishonored."* Titus 2:4b-5

I salute you. However, there are some of you with a chip on your shoulder. You have expectations of this young wife she may not be aware of. You have been a daughter-in-law before and have experience. Give her a break and keep in mind she's new at being an in-law. Give her time to gain life experiences without feeling judged. I believe it was the actress Bette Davis who said, "Old age is not for sissies." How true! Try not to be hurt by disrespect. And PRAY!

> *"Never pay back evil for evil to anyone. Respect what is right in the sight of all men. If possible, so far as it depends on you, be at peace with all men."* Romans 12:17-18

**Question: What practical steps can I make to honor my mother-in-law and move toward a better relationship?**

You've made the first step by desiring more. Good for you! Most people today, especially the younger generation, lead terribly busy lives. An invitation to lunch, just the two of you, would be a great start. I know Mimi loves to go to lunch with her girlfriends so I would see this invitation as moving our relationship to the girlfriend level. If you are a little worried that she may think you have ulterior motives, tell her you are considering this restaurant for a special dinner for your husband's birthday and want her thoughts. This could also open a topic of conversation during your lunch. Ask her about special birthday parties when your husband was a child. What was a special gift he received or the story of a special friend he invited?

Show interest in your mother-in-law. Ask advice on a simple matter and try to implement her advice. It's important you choose a simple matter and not one you cannot follow through on in good conscience. May I propose two to get you started?

- **"What was his favorite meal when he was a boy?"** Mimi asked me a similar question early in their marriage. Marty loved the chocolate cake I used to make for his birthday so she asked for the recipe. I had to confess to her I used a box cake mix but made my own chocolate fudge icing. She was thrilled to have the icing recipe, but every time she tried to make it she had to call me for help. She felt she was a burden, but I loved to know she was trying and desired my help. Annually, we would laugh about all the effort that went into making this cake for him year after year. She would end the conversation with, "I think I have it this time."

- **"I'm going shopping for a new shirt for him. I like how he looks in the color blue but I was wondering if there was a color you thought always looked good on him?"** This question shows you value her opinion and is a win-win. Although, you must remember to tell her what you found and how right she was, he does look great in periwinkle. (Jean humor)

There are also some thoughtful gestures you can make that will mean so much:

- Find a funny card at the store and mail it to her even if you live in the same town. Tell her this card made you laugh and you thought she might enjoy it, too. Everyone likes to receive something beside bills and advertisements in the mail.
- If you live nearby, pick up an extra basket of strawberries or a small bouquet of flowers while you are at the store and drop them off on your way home just so she knows you were thinking about her.
- Find some way to compliment her every time you see her.

**Question: How do I have a good relationship with my daughter-in-law who has held a grudge against me for a misunderstanding that took place years ago?**

Even though Jesus told us to forgive, not seven times, but seventy times seven, some people have a hard time forgiving even once. We all make mistakes for which we need forgiveness. It is our responsibility to seek out the offended, offer a sincere apology and ask for that pardon. Have you offered a sincere apology or discussed the matter with her? One of the points in our in-law seminar was the need to be humble to walk in a manner worthy of our calling as believers in Christ. Ephesians 4 proclaims our walk must be "with all humility." Misunderstandings have a way of distorting the true events of a situation. We must ask ourselves if there is any way we could be wrong. Was there some move on my part, perceived differently than intended? Did that perception become the other person's reality of who I am?

Have you ever been offered an apology like this: "I'm sorry you were offended by what I said."? That is not an apology but transferring the blame to the offended rather than taking responsibility for the offense. A sincere apology should contain accountability for the wrong, understanding that it was hurtful and a desire for reconciliation through the offended's forgiveness. Beyond that, the result is up to that person.

Sometimes a heartfelt note written, once the emotion of the fault has cooled, is a good idea. Again, it should be genuine with sentiment of sorrow and hope of healing and not accusatory or full of excuses. An action that seems silly to us may be of great importance to another. It could be the last straw that released pent-up resentment and caused a volcanic eruption.

It is never too late to offer an apology. If it has been years, then apologize for taking too long to seek forgiveness. It is the Lord you are accountable to and will have to give an answer to one day. Do what you can now by carefully observing whether your pride has played a part in the problem. And PRAY!

**Question: My in-laws continue to voice their opinions about our rearing children. Their ideas are different from ours. How do we handle their unsolicited advice?**

Beliefs about effective child-rearing have changed in the last fifty years and continue to change. We spanked when our boys were little but now we are told not to. In twenty years we may find a swat on the rear was indeed the right thing to do, who knows? Most grandparents mean well and love their grand-children so much its hard not to want to participate in the methods of raising them.

However, some grandparents may be overly critical and see their adult children as immature or incompetent regardless of the fact they are successful married adults. I would encourage you to listen to the advice of everyone who loves your children and has their best interest at heart. This would include doctors, teachers, relatives and close friends. You haven't been a parent before. Keep in mind the grandparents have seen a lot of kids go bad and probably are aware of some common mistakes that contributed to those problems. It might behoove you to listen to their concerns without thinking you are under attack. Ask them a few questions in response to clarify their objections. Have they personally experienced this issue and learned the hard way? Maybe they see some oversight in methods they tried and want to be sure you don't make those same mistakes. After listening, be sure to say you appreciate their concern and you and your husband will discuss their ideas. You will need to express that ultimately you have to do what you feel is right as the parents. You may end up being wrong, but if you are united as a couple and PRAY, God will help you choose the path He wants you to follow.

Oh, dear friends, there is so much to be thankful for in this world. Look around you. Yes, right now, look around you. What one thing do you see that you can say to the Lord, "Thank you?" Is it that you have a roof over your head or food in your refrigerator? Perhaps it's the knowledge your child is healthy or your husband is employed. Take time to savor special moments in your life. Trials have purpose in God's plan. Ask Him for help and while you are waiting, remember to love with an arm around shoulder and a hand over mouth.

*Love,*
*Jean*

CPSIA information can be obtained
at www.ICGtesting.com
Printed in the USA
BVHW08s0258121018
529906BV00002B/399/P